D1711359

51st Edition

Travel to Minneapolis, Minnesota

2023
People Who Know
Publishing
Jack Ross

I

People Who Know Publishing

Forward: In this book, People Who Know Publishing will provide a travel guide of 101+ things to see, do and visit in Minneapolis, Minnesota. We strive to make our guides as comprehensive and complete as possible. We publish travel guides on cities and countries all over the world. Feel free to check out our complete list of travel guides here:

People Who Know Publishing partners with local experts to produce travel guides on various locations. We differentiate ourselves from other travel books by focusing on areas not typically covered by others. Our guides include a detailed history of the location and its population. In addition to covering all of the "must see" areas of a location such as museums and local sights, we also provide up-to-date restaurant suggestions and local food traditions.

To make a request for a travel guide on a particular area or to join our email list to stay updated on travel tips from local experts sign up here: https://mailchi.mp/c74b62620b1f/travel-books

Be sure to confirm restaurants, addresses, and phone numbers as those may have changed since the book was published.

About the Author:

Jack Ross is a college student who was born in Westchester County, NY. He's an expert on the local "in the know" tips of the area and is an authority on Westchester and its towns. He's been featured in several publications including Business Insider and CNBC for his books.

During his spare time, he writes, plays tennis and golf and enjoys all water sports (including his latest favorite, the eFoil). Jack also enjoys traveling and is a food connoisseur throughout Westchester. Jack travels consistently and has been to majority of the states in the U.S.

Sign up for our email list to get inside access to the towns and places we cover!
>> https://mailchi.mp/c74b62620b1f/travel-books
>> https://mailchi.mp/c74b62620b1f/travel-books

Table of Contents

State: California
Population: 429,606
Ranking in U.S.: N/A
County: Hennepin County
Founded: 1856
Tag line: N/A

Minneapolis, Minnesota

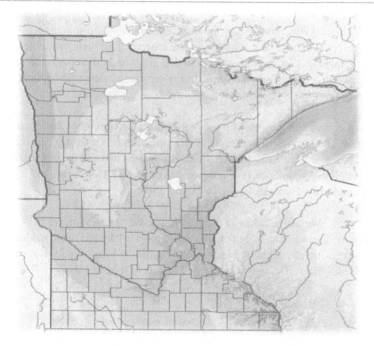

Introduction

"Minneapolis is a city that feels like a big city but has that small-town charm." - Lizzo, Grammy-winning musician and Minneapolis native.

Minneapolis, often referred to as the "City of Lakes," is a captivating metropolis situated in the heart of the American Midwest. As one half of the celebrated "Twin Cities" alongside its sibling city, St. Paul, Minneapolis is a dynamic and culturally rich urban hub that boasts a unique blend of modernity and small-town charm.

With a history dating back to its founding in the mid-19th century, Minneapolis has evolved from a milling and industrial center along the scenic banks of the Mississippi River to become a thriving, diverse, and innovative city. Its transformation over the decades has been nothing short of remarkable.

One of the defining features of Minneapolis is its exquisite natural beauty. The city is famously known for its abundance of lakes, including Lake Calhoun, Lake Harriet, and Lake of the Isles, which provide picturesque backdrops for outdoor activities, from boating and swimming in the summer to ice skating in the winter. These urban oases create a serene contrast to the bustling cityscape, earning Minneapolis its "City of Lakes" moniker.

Beyond its natural attractions, Minneapolis is a testament to the concept of "Minnesota Nice." The residents of the city are renowned for their friendliness and hospitality, making it an inviting and welcoming place for both visitors and newcomers. This sense of community is deeply ingrained in the city's culture, fostering an atmosphere of inclusivity and neighborly camaraderie.

In terms of culture and the arts, Minneapolis boasts a thriving scene that rivals much larger cities. The Minneapolis Institute of Arts, the Walker Art Center, and the Guthrie Theater are just a few of the cultural institutions that call the city home. Music also plays a significant role in the city's identity, with legendary musicians like Prince and Bob Dylan hailing from Minneapolis.

In recent years, Minneapolis has gained recognition for its commitment to sustainability, green living, and urban development. The city has made strides in promoting eco-friendly initiatives and creating walkable, bike-friendly neighborhoods that reflect the changing preferences of its residents.

History

European Settlement: The first European presence in the area dates back to the late 1600s when French fur traders and explorers began to arrive. In the early 19th century, the United States gained control of the region through treaties with Native American tribes.

Milling and Industry: Minneapolis's growth was catalyzed by the milling industry. The city's location along the Mississippi River and the presence of St. Anthony Falls provided abundant waterpower for mills. In the mid-1800s, sawmills, flour mills, and textile mills sprang up, earning Minneapolis the nickname "Mill City."

Native American Roots: Long before European settlers arrived, the land where Minneapolis now stands was inhabited by the Dakota Sioux people. The Dakota people called the region "Bdóte," meaning "the meeting place of waters," which referred to the confluence of the Mississippi and Minnesota Rivers.

Travel to Minneapolis Minnesota

City Incorporation: Minneapolis was officially incorporated as a city on March 6, 1856. During this time, it was a bustling industrial center, attracting immigrants from Europe and migrants from other parts of the United States.

Flour Milling Capital: By the late 19th century, Minneapolis had become the flour milling capital of the world, thanks in part to innovations like the invention of the roller mill. Flour milling was so vital to the city's economy that it led to the formation of major milling companies like Pillsbury and General Mills.

Growth and Diversification: In the early 20th century, Minneapolis continued to grow and diversify its economy. It became a center for finance, commerce, and industry, with a thriving theater and arts scene.

Modern Minneapolis: In recent decades, Minneapolis has continued to evolve. It is known for its vibrant music scene, with artists like Prince and Bob Dylan emerging from the city. The Guthrie Theater, Walker Art Center, and Minneapolis Institute of Arts are cultural landmarks.

Contemporary Challenges: Minneapolis has faced challenges, including issues related to racial disparities, economic inequality, and, notably, the protests and unrest following the death of George Floyd in 2020, which brought international attention to issues of racial justice and policing.

Economy

Minneapolis has a diverse and robust economy characterized by a mix of industries and sectors that contribute to its overall prosperity. Here's an overview of its economic landscape:

Minneapolis is a major financial center in the Midwest, with several prominent financial institutions headquartered in the city, including Wells Fargo, U.S. Bancorp, and Ameriprise Financial.

The city's economy has a strong presence in the healthcare and medical technology sectors, with the Mayo Clinic and the University of Minnesota Medical Center being significant contributors.

The technology and software industries have been on the rise in Minneapolis, with a growing number of startups and established tech companies, particularly in fields such as software development, data analytics, and medical technology.

Manufacturing, historically tied to the city's milling heritage, remains an important part of Minneapolis's economy, with companies engaged in food processing, machinery, and other manufacturing activities.

Minneapolis's status as a major transportation hub is supported by a thriving logistics and transportation sector, including major companies in the trucking and freight industries.

The city's retail and consumer goods sector is bolstered by the presence of major retailers, including Target Corporation, which is headquartered in nearby Minneapolis suburb Minneapolis boasts a strong arts and culture scene, contributing to its economy through theaters, galleries, and music venues.

Education and research institutions, including the University of Minnesota and several colleges and universities, are significant economic drivers in the region.

Tourism plays a role in Minneapolis's economy, with visitors drawn to attractions such as the Mall of America, professional sports teams, and cultural events.

Minneapolis has a diverse workforce with a focus on education and innovation, contributing to its reputation as a hub for talent and creativity.

Transportation Systems

Roads and Highways: Minneapolis has an extensive network of roads and highways, making it easily accessible by car. Major highways that pass through or near the city include Interstate 94 (I-94), Interstate 35W (I-35W), Interstate 394 (I-394), and Interstate 494 (I-494).

Public Transit: The Metro Transit system operates buses and light rail transit (LRT) services in the Minneapolis-St. Paul metropolitan area. The METRO Blue Line and METRO Green Line are two LRT lines that connect Minneapolis with its neighboring city, St. Paul, as well as with several suburbs. The city also has a comprehensive bus network serving various neighborhoods.

Bicycling: Minneapolis is known for its bike-friendly infrastructure and commitment to cycling. The city has an extensive network of bike lanes, trails, and dedicated bike-sharing programs. The Nice Ride Minnesota program, for example, offers bike rentals at various locations throughout the city.

Walking: Minneapolis is a pedestrian-friendly city, with many neighborhoods designed for walkability. Sidewalks and pedestrian-friendly streets make it easy for residents and visitors to explore the city on foot.

Airports: Minneapolis-Saint Paul International Airport (MSP) is the major airport serving the region. It's located southwest of downtown Minneapolis and offers both domestic and international flights.

Amtrak: The Minneapolis-Saint Paul area is served by Amtrak's Empire Builder train route, which connects the city to other major cities, including Chicago and Seattle.

Car Sharing and Ride-Sharing: Car-sharing services like Zipcar and ride-sharing services like Uber and Lyft are widely available in Minneapolis, providing additional transportation options.

Parking: Minneapolis provides a range of parking options, including street parking, parking ramps, and surface lots, to accommodate both residents and visitors. Some areas may require payment for parking.

Bridges: Due to its location along the Mississippi River, Minneapolis is known for its numerous bridges. The Stone Arch Bridge is a historic pedestrian and bicycle bridge that offers scenic views of the river and the city skyline.

Neighborhoods

Downtown Minneapolis: The heart of the city, downtown Minneapolis offers a bustling urban environment with numerous restaurants, shops, theaters, and cultural attractions. It's a prime location for professionals, and its housing options range from modern apartments to upscale condos.

Uptown: Known for its trendy vibe, Uptown is a popular neighborhood with a vibrant arts and music scene, hip boutiques, and a wide range of dining options. It's especially attractive to young professionals and those who enjoy a lively atmosphere.

North Loop: This former warehouse district has been revitalized into a chic and trendy neighborhood. It's home to upscale boutiques, art galleries, and some of the city's finest restaurants. North Loop also offers loft-style living spaces.

Loring Park: Located near downtown, Loring Park is a picturesque neighborhood known for its green spaces, including Loring Park itself. It's a residential area with a mix of housing options, from historic homes to modern apartments.

Northeast Minneapolis (Nordeast): This artsy and diverse neighborhood is known for its craft breweries, art studios, and historic architecture. It's a popular area for those seeking a vibrant arts scene and unique dining experiences.

Southwest Minneapolis (Linden Hills and Kingfield): These residential neighborhoods offer a quieter, family-friendly atmosphere with tree-lined streets and local businesses. They are known for their strong sense of community and are popular with families.

Food

Juicy Lucy: A Minneapolis invention, the Juicy Lucy is a cheese-stuffed burger where the cheese is hidden inside the patty. Two popular spots to try this iconic burger are Matt's Bar and the 5-8 Club.

Norwegian and Scandinavian Cuisine: Given the city's Scandinavian heritage, you'll find delicious Nordic dishes like lefse (potato flatbread), lutefisk, Swedish meatballs, and herring at various restaurants.

Farm-to-Table Fare: Minneapolis has a strong commitment to local, sustainable, and organic food. Explore farm-to-table restaurants that offer seasonal dishes made from fresh, locally sourced ingredients.

Cultural Diversity: The city's diverse population means you can savor cuisines from around the world. Explore neighborhoods like Eat Street (Nicollet Avenue) for international flavors, including Vietnamese, Thai, Mexican, Ethiopian, and more.

Craft Beer and Brewpubs: Minneapolis has a thriving craft beer scene with numerous breweries and brewpubs offering a wide range of beer styles. Many of these establishments also serve delicious pub food and snacks.

Northwoods Cuisine: Experience dishes inspired by Minnesota's northern wilderness, such as wild rice soup, walleye (a popular local fish), and dishes featuring locally foraged ingredients.

Here are our ten favorite restaurant recommendations!

1.Spoon and Stable: Chef Gavin Kaysen's restaurant in a beautifully restored stable offers a seasonal and locally sourced menu with a focus on French cuisine and contemporary twists.

2.Young Joni: Known for its wood-fired pizzas and inventive small plates, Young Joni by Chef Ann Kim is a trendy spot offering a cozy atmosphere and a unique cocktail program.

3.Gardens of Salonica: This beloved Minneapolis restaurant serves authentic Greek cuisine in a warm and welcoming atmosphere. The menu features classic dishes like moussaka, souvlaki, and baklava.

4.Bachelor Farmer: A Nordic-inspired restaurant with an emphasis on local ingredients, Bachelor Farmer offers a farm-to-table dining experience with a Scandinavian twist.

5.Birch's on the Lake: Located on the shores of Long Lake, Birch's offers upscale dining along with its own brewery. The menu includes a variety of dishes, from seafood to steak.

6.Manny's Steakhouse: A Minneapolis institution, Manny's is known for its prime steaks and an extensive wine list. It's a classic steakhouse experience in the heart of the city.

7.Alma: This restaurant offers a tasting menu featuring seasonal ingredients and modern American cuisine. It's known for its inventive dishes and an adjoining cafe serving breakfast and lunch.

8.Brasa Premium Rotisserie: Specializing in slow-cooked, rotisserie meats and Southern-inspired sides, Brasa offers a casual yet delicious dining experience with a focus on sustainability.

9.Revival: A destination for southern comfort food, Revival serves up dishes like fried chicken, macaroni and cheese, and collard greens with a modern twist.

10.Pizzeria Lola: A local favorite for pizza, Pizzeria Lola offers a wide range of creative and classic pizza options, including vegetarian and gluten-free choices.

Nightlife

Downtown Minneapolis: The downtown area is a nightlife hub with a wide range of bars, clubs, and entertainment options. You can find everything from upscale cocktail lounges to energetic nightclubs.

Warehouse District/North Loop: This area is home to some of the city's trendiest bars, nightclubs, and restaurants. It's a popular destination for those seeking a lively night out.

Uptown: Uptown offers a mix of bars, breweries, and live music venues. You can enjoy a laid-back evening with craft beers or explore venues with live bands and DJ sets.

Northeast Minneapolis: This artsy neighborhood has a growing nightlife scene, with bars and breweries often featuring local art and live music. It's a great place to explore for a more eclectic experience.

Live Music Venues: Minneapolis is known for its live music scene, and venues like First Avenue, the Turf Club, and the Dakota Jazz Club regularly host concerts by local and national artists across various genres.

Craft Breweries: If you're a craft beer enthusiast, Minneapolis has numerous breweries and taprooms where you can enjoy locally brewed beers in a relaxed atmosphere. Places like Surly Brewing Co. and Dangerous Man Brewing Co. are popular choices.

Local Traditions & Customs

Minnesota Nice: "Minnesota Nice" is a widely recognized custom that refers to the friendliness, politeness, and courtesy of Minnesotans. People in Minneapolis are generally warm and welcoming, and it's common to greet strangers with a smile and engage in friendly conversations.

Outdoor Activities: Given its abundance of lakes, parks, and natural beauty, outdoor activities are a cherished tradition in Minneapolis. From ice fishing in the winter to boating and biking in the summer, many residents take advantage of the city's natural resources year-round.

Lakes and Cabin Culture: Owning a cabin in the northern woods of Minnesota is a cherished tradition for many Minneapolis residents. The "up north" cabin culture involves escaping to secluded cabins for weekends and holidays to enjoy nature, fishing, and relaxation.

Winter Sports: With its cold winters, Minneapolis embraces winter sports traditions. Ice skating, cross-country skiing, and snowmobiling are popular winter activities, and many Minnesotans take pride in their ability to endure and enjoy the winter season.

State Fair: The Minnesota State Fair, held in nearby St. Paul, is a beloved tradition for many Minneapolis residents. It's one of the largest state fairs in the United States and features a wide range of food, entertainment, and agricultural exhibits.

Hot Dish: "Hot dish" is a traditional Minnesota casserole dish often made with ground meat, vegetables, and a starch like tater tots or pasta, all baked together in a creamy sauce. It's a comfort food staple in many households.

What to buy?

Local Art and Crafts: Minneapolis has a thriving arts scene, and you can find unique and locally made art and crafts at galleries and art markets. Look for paintings, sculptures, pottery, and other handcrafted items.

Minneapolis Apparel: Show your Minneapolis pride by purchasing clothing or accessories with the city's name or iconic landmarks. Local shops often carry Minneapolis-themed T-shirts, hoodies, and caps.

Jewelry: Minneapolis has several jewelry stores and artisans who create beautiful pieces. Consider buying a unique necklace, bracelet, or pair of earrings as a keepsake or gift.

Local Food and Drink: Minnesota is known for its specialty foods, such as wild rice, maple syrup, and gourmet chocolates. Visit local markets or specialty shops to find these items, which make great gifts or souvenirs.

Craft Beer and Spirits: Minneapolis has a burgeoning craft beer and distillery scene. Look for locally brewed beers, spirits, or even a growler filled with your favorite brew to take home.

Local Books: Minneapolis has a strong literary tradition. Browse local bookstores for books by Minnesota authors, including works of fiction, non-fiction, and poetry.

Musical Instruments and Records: Minneapolis has a rich musical heritage, and you can find musical instruments, vinyl records, and CDs at independent music stores. Look for music from local artists, such as Prince or Bob Dylan.

Finally, here are the five most famous people from the city!

Prince (Prince Rogers Nelson): The iconic musician and songwriter Prince was born and raised in Minneapolis. He became a global superstar known for his innovative music, distinctive style, and hits like "Purple Rain," "When Doves Cry," and "Kiss."

Bob Dylan (Robert Zimmerman): Although born in Duluth, Minnesota, Bob Dylan spent a significant part of his early career in Minneapolis. He is one of the most influential figures in the history of American music, known for his folk and rock songs, including "Blowin' in the Wind" and "Like a Rolling Stone."

Charles Schulz: The beloved cartoonist, best known for creating the "Peanuts" comic strip featuring characters like Charlie Brown, Snoopy, and Linus, was born in Minneapolis. His work has had a lasting impact on popular culture.

Hubert H. Humphrey: A prominent politician, Hubert Humphrey served as the Vice President of the United States under President Lyndon B. Johnson from 1965 to 1969. He also had a long and influential career in the U.S. Senate, where he represented Minnesota.

Garrison Keillor: A well-known author, storyteller, and radio host, Garrison Keillor is best known for his radio program, "A Prairie Home Companion," which showcased humor, music, and storytelling with a Midwestern flair. The show was based in St. Paul but had strong ties to Minneapolis as well.

101+ things to do in the city

1. Visit the Minneapolis Institute of Arts.
2. Explore the Walker Art Center.
3. Attend a performance at the Guthrie Theater.
4. Check out the Weisman Art Museum.
5. Enjoy live music at First Avenue.
6. Attend a concert by the Minnesota Orchestra.
7. Explore the American Swedish Institute.
8. Visit the Mill City Museum.
9. Experience local theater at the Mixed Blood Theatre.
10. Explore the Minneapolis Sculpture Garden.
11. Bike or walk around Lake Calhoun (Bde Maka Ska).
12. Go for a hike in Minnehaha Regional Park.
13. Canoe or kayak on the Chain of Lakes.
14. Play golf at one of the city's golf courses.
15. Visit the Eloise Butler Wildflower Garden and Bird Sanctuary.
16. Take a Segway tour along the riverfront.
17. Go ice skating at The Depot's indoor rink.
18. Explore the Como Park Zoo and Conservatory in nearby St. Paul.
19. Enjoy a day of fishing on the Mississippi River.
20. Go cross-country skiing in Theodore Wirth Regional Park.
21. Try a Juicy Lucy burger at Matt's Bar.
22. Sample Scandinavian cuisine at Fika.
23. Dine at Spoon and Stable for a fine dining experience.
24. Enjoy farm-to-table dining at The Bachelor Farmer.
25. Have brunch at Hell's Kitchen.
26. Savor a meal at Manny's Steakhouse.
27. Taste local craft beer at Surly Brewing Company.
28. Experience Middle Eastern cuisine at Holy Land.
29. Visit the Midtown Global Market for international foods.
30. Explore local food trucks for diverse culinary delights.
31. Catch a live comedy show at Acme Comedy Co.
32. Dance the night away at The Exchange & Alibi Lounge.
33. Attend a live music show at Icehouse.
34. Enjoy karaoke at The Shout! House.
35. Play arcade games at Up-Down Minneapolis.
36. Try your luck at Mystic Lake Casino.
37. Attend a sports game at Target Field or U.S. Bank Stadium.
38. Experience the nightlife in the North Loop district.
39. Check out a burlesque show at Lush Bar.
40. Explore the craft cocktail scene at Marvel Bar.

41.Tour the Minneapolis Central Library.

42.Learn about the city's milling history at the Mill City Museum.

43.Visit the Minnesota History Center in St. Paul.

44.Explore the Somali Museum of Minnesota.

45.Discover the Bakken Museum of Electricity.

46.Learn about Minnesota's Jewish history at the Jewish Historical Society of the Upper Midwest.

47.Visit the Hennepin History Museum.

48.Explore the Firefighters Hall and Museum.

49.Discover the history of music at the Schubert Club Museum.

50.Tour the Wells Fargo History Museum.

51.Shop for local goods at the Minneapolis Farmers Market.

52.Explore the Mall of America for shopping and entertainment.

53.Visit the Midtown Global Market for unique items.

54.Stroll through the North Loop's boutique shops.

55.Shop for vintage finds at Rewind Minneapolis.

56.Explore the locally owned stores on Nicollet Avenue.

57.Check out the Minneapolis Craft Market.

58.Visit the Minneapolis Convention Center's gift shops.

59.Explore the boutiques in the Uptown neighborhood.

60.Hunt for antiques at Hunt & Gather.

61.Picnic in Boom Island Park.

62.Visit the Eloise Butler Wildflower Garden.

63.Relax in Gold Medal Park.

64.Go birdwatching in the Cedar Lake Wildlife Area.

65.Play frisbee golf at Bryant Lake Regional Park.

66.Explore the scenic Minnehaha Falls Park.

67.Have a barbecue in Lake Harriet Park.

68.Take a leisurely walk in Theodore Wirth Regional Park.

69.Visit the Lyndale Park Rose Garden.

70.Enjoy the views from the Stone Arch Bridge Park.

71.Explore the Bakken Museum of Electricity.

72.Visit the Bell Museum of Natural History.

73.Discover the Raptor Center at the University of Minnesota.

74.Take a riverboat cruise on the Mississippi River.

75.Explore the Science Museum of Minnesota in St. Paul.

76.Go stargazing at the Minneapolis Planetarium.

77.Visit the Minnesota Zoo in nearby Apple Valley.

78.Learn about marine life at SEA LIFE at Mall of America.

79.Attend a nature program at Eloise Butler Wildflower Garden.

80.Explore the Mississippi National River and Recreation Area.

81.Visit the Minnesota Children's Museum in St. Paul.

82.Explore the Como Park Zoo and Conservatory.

83.Enjoy a day at Valleyfair amusement park.

84.Go indoor rock climbing at Vertical Endeavors.

85.Visit the Science Museum of Minnesota.

86.Have a family picnic in Minnehaha Regional Park.

87.Explore the Sea Life Minnesota Aquarium.

88.Attend a Minnesota Twins baseball game.

89.Go horseback riding at Bunker Park Stable.

90.Take a paddlewheel riverboat tour on the Mississippi.

91.Attend the Minnesota State Fair in nearby St. Paul.

92.Experience the Minneapolis Aquatennial celebration.

93.Enjoy the Minneapolis St. Paul International Film Festival.

94.Attend the Minneapolis Pride Festival.

95.Celebrate the Holidazzle Festival during the holiday season.

96.Visit the Uptown Art Fair.

97.Attend the Stone Arch Bridge Festival.

98.Experience the Minneapolis Fringe Festival.

99.Participate in the Twin Cities Marathon.

100.Attend the MayDay Parade and Festival.

101.Take a hot air balloon ride over the city.

102.Explore the Minneapolis Skyway System.

103.Go indoor skydiving at iFLY Minneapolis.

104.Take a brewery tour at a local craft brewery.

105.Try your hand at ax throwing at a local venue.

106.Visit the Minnesota Transportation Museum.

107.Attend a live radio show taping at WCCO Radio.

108.Go on a brewery and distillery tour.

109.Explore the Minnesota Landscape Arboretum in nearby Chanhassen.

110.Take a scenic river cruise on the Mississippi River.

1.Visit the Minneapolis Institute of Arts.

The Minneapolis Institute of Arts (MIA) is a renowned and highly respected art museum located in Minneapolis, Minnesota. It is one of the largest art museums in the United States and is known for its impressive and diverse collection of art spanning various cultures, time periods, and artistic styles.

Collection: The MIA's permanent collection comprises over 90,000 works of art, including paintings, sculptures, textiles, decorative arts, photographs, and more. The collection encompasses art from all over the world, with a particular emphasis on European, American, Asian, and African art. Visitors can explore pieces by celebrated artists such as Vincent van Gogh, Rembrandt, Georgia O'Keeffe, and Pablo Picasso.

Galleries: The museum's galleries are thoughtfully organized, allowing visitors to journey through different cultures and art movements. You can explore ancient Egyptian artifacts, European masterpieces, contemporary art, and so much more within its well-curated exhibition spaces.

Special Exhibitions: In addition to its permanent collection, the MIA hosts a rotating schedule of special exhibitions. These exhibitions often feature art on loan from other museums and private collections, providing fresh and unique experiences for visitors.

Educational Programs: The MIA is committed to education and offers a wide range of programs for visitors of all ages. These include guided tours, art classes, workshops, lectures, and family-friendly activities. The museum aims to engage and inspire the community through art.

Architecture: The museum's building itself is a work of art. Designed by the architectural firm McKim, Mead & White, the neoclassical structure features a stunning façade, a grand entrance hall, and elegant galleries that enhance the overall museum experience.

Accessibility: The MIA strives to be accessible to all visitors. It offers resources for individuals with disabilities, including wheelchair accessibility, assistive listening devices, and accessible tours.

Dining and Shopping: The museum has on-site dining options, including a café and a restaurant, where visitors can enjoy a meal or a snack. There's also a museum shop where you can purchase art-related books, gifts, and souvenirs.

Events: The MIA hosts various events throughout the year, including lectures, concerts, and cultural festivals. These events provide opportunities for visitors to immerse themselves in the world of art and culture.

Membership: The museum offers membership options for individuals and families, providing benefits such as free admission, exclusive previews, and discounts at the museum shop and café.

The Minneapolis Institute of Arts is a cultural gem in the city, offering an enriching and inspiring experience for art enthusiasts, students, families, and anyone interested in exploring the world of art. Its commitment to education, diverse collections, and engaging exhibitions make it a must-visit destination for both residents and visitors to Minneapolis.

2.Explore the Walker Art Center.

The Walker Art Center is a renowned contemporary art museum located in Minneapolis, Minnesota. It is known for its cutting-edge exhibitions, innovative programming, and a striking architectural design. Here's an exploration of what you can expect when visiting the Walker Art Center:

Contemporary Art: The Walker is dedicated to showcasing contemporary art in all its forms, including visual arts, performing arts, film, and more. It features a dynamic collection of works by both established and emerging artists, making it a hub for artistic innovation.

The Collection: While the Walker Art Center primarily focuses on rotating exhibitions, it also has a notable collection of contemporary art. The collection includes works by artists such as Andy Warhol, Jasper Johns, Cindy Sherman, and Yoko Ono, among others. You can explore these pieces in various media, including paintings, sculptures, photography, and video art.

Exhibitions: The Walker hosts a diverse range of exhibitions that push the boundaries of contemporary art. From solo shows featuring influential artists to thematic exhibitions that address pressing social and cultural issues, there's always something thought-provoking and visually stimulating on display.

Sculpture Garden: Adjacent to the museum is the Minneapolis Sculpture Garden, one of the most iconic outdoor art spaces in the city. It's home to the famous "Spoonbridge and Cherry" sculpture, among other striking pieces. The garden is a serene place to explore and relax, with sculptures set against a backdrop of beautiful landscaping.

Performing Arts: In addition to visual art, the Walker is known for its commitment to the performing arts. It hosts dance performances, music concerts, theater productions, and other live events in its state-of-the-art McGuire Theater. These performances often challenge traditional notions of art and offer a multidisciplinary experience.

Film and Media: The Walker Art Center's cinema is dedicated to screening independent and avant-garde films. It hosts film festivals, retrospectives, and screenings of classic and contemporary cinema, making it a destination for cinephiles.

Walker Shop: The museum's shop offers a curated selection of art books, unique gifts, and contemporary design objects. It's a great place to find souvenirs or gifts inspired by the world of art.

Café and Dining: The Walker Art Center features a café where you can grab a bite to eat or enjoy a cup of coffee. The cuisine is often locally sourced and reflects the creative spirit of the museum.

Accessibility: The museum strives to be accessible to all visitors, providing services such as wheelchair accessibility, guided tours, and assistive listening devices.

Educational Programs: The Walker offers educational programs for visitors of all ages, including guided tours, workshops, lectures, and hands-on art activities.

Membership: Becoming a member of the Walker Art Center offers benefits such as free admission to exhibitions, exclusive access to events, and discounts on performances and programs.

The Walker Art Center is a vibrant cultural institution that pushes the boundaries of contemporary art and creativity. Whether you're an art enthusiast, a fan of experimental performances, or simply curious about the cutting edge of culture, a visit to the Walker promises an engaging and inspiring experience.

3.Attend a performance at the Guthrie Theater.

The Guthrie Theater is a world-renowned regional theater located in Minneapolis, Minnesota. It is known for its exceptional productions, commitment to the performing arts, and striking architectural design. Here's what you can expect when attending a performance at the Guthrie Theater:

Theater Complex: The Guthrie Theater is housed in a visually stunning, modernist building designed by architect Jean Nouvel. The building itself is a work of art and offers panoramic views of the Mississippi River and the city skyline from its cantilevered balconies.

Performance Spaces: The Guthrie has three main performance spaces:

Wurtele Thrust Stage: This is the largest stage and the most versatile. It features a thrust stage that extends into the audience, creating an intimate and immersive theater experience.
McGuire Proscenium Stage: A more traditional proscenium stage, this space is often used for classic plays and larger-scale productions.
Dowling Studio: An intimate black-box theater that hosts experimental and smaller productions, as well as performances by emerging artists.
Diverse Productions: The Guthrie Theater presents a wide range of productions, including classic plays, contemporary dramas, musicals, and experimental works. Its repertoire includes works by renowned playwrights, both new and established.

Talented Actors: The Guthrie attracts some of the most talented actors, directors, and designers from across the country and around the world. Performances feature a combination of local actors and guest artists, resulting in high-quality productions.

Educational Programs: The theater is committed to education and offers a variety of programs for students and the community. These include workshops, classes, and opportunities to engage with the creative process.

Accessible Performances: The Guthrie strives to make theater accessible to all audiences. It offers services such as captioning, audio description, and sensory-friendly performances for individuals with disabilities.

Membership: Becoming a member of the Guthrie Theater offers benefits such as priority ticket access, discounts on additional tickets, and invitations to special events.

Dining: The Guthrie features on-site dining options where you can enjoy a meal or drinks before or after the performance. These options often incorporate locally sourced ingredients and offer a variety of menu choices.

Cultural Hub: In addition to its performances, the Guthrie serves as a cultural hub in Minneapolis. It hosts discussions, forums, and events that engage the community in conversations about art, culture, and social issues.

Scenic Views: While at the Guthrie, take some time to enjoy the breathtaking views of the Mississippi River and the Stone Arch Bridge from the building's cantilevered balconies and observation decks.

Attending a performance at the Guthrie Theater is not only an opportunity to enjoy world-class theater but also to immerse yourself in the vibrant arts and culture scene of Minneapolis. The theater's commitment to artistic excellence and innovation ensures that every visit is a memorable and enriching experience.

4.Check out the Weisman Art Museum.

The Weisman Art Museum, located in Minneapolis, Minnesota, is a distinctive and architecturally striking institution that specializes in American modern and contemporary art. Here's what you can expect when you visit the Weisman Art Museum:

Architectural Marvel: The Weisman Art Museum building itself is a work of art. Designed by renowned architect Frank Gehry, the museum's unique and avant-garde architecture features stainless steel cladding, whimsical angles, and bold shapes. It's often described as a "modernist sculpture."

Art Collection: The Weisman's collection focuses primarily on American art from the early 20th century to the present day. You'll find a diverse array of artworks, including paintings, sculptures, prints, drawings, and decorative arts. The collection includes pieces by notable artists such as Georgia O'Keeffe, Marsden Hartley, and Alfred Maurer.

Contemporary Art: While the museum's collection encompasses a wide range of American art, it has a particular emphasis on contemporary works. It frequently showcases innovative and thought-provoking art, making it a dynamic destination for those interested in the cutting edge of the art world.

Special Exhibitions: In addition to its permanent collection, the Weisman Art Museum hosts rotating special exhibitions. These exhibitions often feature works by emerging and established artists, offering fresh perspectives and engaging experiences for visitors.

Educational Programs: The museum is dedicated to education and offers a variety of programs for visitors of all ages. These include guided tours, lectures, workshops, and interactive activities that encourage exploration and creativity.

Accessibility: The Weisman strives to be accessible to all visitors, providing services such as wheelchair accessibility, assistive listening devices, and tours designed for individuals with disabilities.

Café and Museum Shop: The museum has an on-site café where you can grab a snack or a coffee, and a museum shop offering art-related books, gifts, and souvenirs.

Events: The Weisman Art Museum hosts events throughout the year, including exhibition openings, lectures, and art-related gatherings. These events provide opportunities for visitors to engage with the local art community and gain deeper insights into the world of art.

Membership: Becoming a member of the Weisman Art Museum offers benefits such as free admission, exclusive access to events, and discounts on programs and merchandise.

Outdoor Sculpture Garden: Adjacent to the museum is the Frederick R. Weisman Art Museum's Sculpture Garden. It features a selection of outdoor sculptures, providing a unique blend of art and nature.

A visit to the Weisman Art Museum is not only an opportunity to appreciate outstanding American art but also to marvel at the architectural wonder of the building itself. Whether you're an art enthusiast, an architecture aficionado, or simply looking for a culturally enriching experience, the Weisman Art Museum offers a unique and inspiring destination in Minneapolis.

5.Enjoy live music at First Avenue.

First Avenue is a legendary music venue and nightclub located in Minneapolis, Minnesota. It has played a pivotal role in the city's music scene and is renowned for hosting live music performances across various genres. Here's what you can expect when you enjoy live music at First Avenue:

Music Variety: First Avenue showcases a diverse range of musical genres, including rock, hip-hop, punk, electronic, indie, and more. Whether you're into mainstream acts or emerging artists, you'll find a wide spectrum of musical talent gracing the stage.

Historic Venue: The venue has a rich history and has hosted numerous iconic artists and bands over the years. It gained international recognition when it was featured prominently in the film "Purple Rain" starring Prince, who is closely associated with the venue.

Multiple Stages: First Avenue features multiple stages, each with its own unique atmosphere and capacity. The Mainroom is the largest stage and is known for hosting major concerts and events. The 7th St Entry is a smaller, intimate space that often showcases up-and-coming artists.

Live Performances: You can expect an electric and energetic atmosphere at First Avenue concerts. The venue's excellent sound system and lighting enhance the live music experience, making it a favorite among both artists and fans.

Local and National Acts: While First Avenue has hosted countless national and international touring acts, it also supports and promotes local Minnesota musicians. It's a platform where local bands and artists can gain exposure and build their fan base.

Famous Acts: Many famous musicians and bands have performed at First Avenue throughout its history. In addition to Prince, artists like Bob Dylan, The Replacements, Nirvana, and U2 have graced its stage.

Dance Nights: First Avenue also hosts dance nights and DJ sets, providing a vibrant nightlife experience for those who love to dance and enjoy electronic and dance music.

Accessibility: The venue is known for its accessibility and welcoming atmosphere, making it a popular choice for music lovers of all backgrounds and ages.

Memorabilia: The walls of First Avenue are adorned with memorabilia from its storied history, including photographs, posters, and other artifacts that pay homage to the musicians who have performed there.

Bars and Refreshments: The venue offers a selection of bars where you can enjoy a wide range of beverages, including craft beers, cocktails, and non-alcoholic options.

Membership: First Avenue offers membership options that can provide benefits such as priority access to tickets, discounts, and exclusive event invitations.

Whether you're a music enthusiast, a fan of live performances, or simply looking for a memorable night out in Minneapolis, enjoying live music at First Avenue is an iconic and thrilling experience that captures the city's vibrant music culture.

6.Attend a concert by the Minnesota Orchestra.

Attending a concert by the Minnesota Orchestra is a cultural and musical experience that offers a chance to enjoy the world-class talent of one of the most esteemed orchestras in the United States. Here's what you can expect when you attend a concert by the Minnesota Orchestra:

Orchestra Excellence: The Minnesota Orchestra is renowned for its exceptional musicianship and artistry. It consists of a talented ensemble of musicians who perform a diverse repertoire, ranging from classical masterpieces to contemporary compositions.

Venue: Concerts by the Minnesota Orchestra are typically held at Orchestra Hall, a beautifully designed and acoustically superb venue located in downtown Minneapolis. The hall's architecture and acoustics enhance the overall concert experience.

Repertoire: The orchestra performs a wide variety of music, including symphonies, concertos, chamber music, and contemporary works. They often collaborate with world-renowned conductors and guest artists, adding depth and diversity to their performances.

Season Programs: The orchestra's concert season is divided into different series, each offering a unique thematic focus. These series may include classical masterworks, pops, family concerts, and special thematic performances.

Guest Artists: Renowned soloists, conductors, and guest artists frequently join the Minnesota Orchestra for performances. These collaborations bring a rich and diverse range of talent to the stage.

Education and Outreach: The orchestra is committed to education and community engagement. It offers a variety of educational programs, including concerts for young audiences, open rehearsals, and initiatives to introduce classical music to a broader audience.

Special Events: In addition to its regular concert series, the Minnesota Orchestra hosts special events, such as holiday concerts, outdoor performances, and collaborations with local arts organizations.

Accessibility: Orchestra Hall is designed to be accessible to all patrons, with accommodations for individuals with disabilities and services like assistive listening devices.

Dining: The venue offers dining options, including a café and bars where you can enjoy refreshments before or after the concert.

Membership and Subscriptions: Becoming a subscriber or member of the Minnesota Orchestra often provides benefits such as priority ticket access, discounts, and invitations to exclusive events.

Cultural Experience: Attending a concert by the Minnesota Orchestra is not just a musical experience; it's also a cultural and artistic journey that allows you to immerse yourself in the beauty and emotional depth of classical music.

Whether you're a seasoned classical music enthusiast or someone looking to explore the world of orchestral music, attending a concert by the Minnesota Orchestra is a memorable and enriching experience that showcases the power and beauty of live symphonic music.

7.Explore the American Swedish Institute.

The American Swedish Institute (ASI) is a cultural center and museum located in Minneapolis, Minnesota, dedicated to celebrating and preserving Swedish and Swedish-American heritage and culture. Here's what you can expect when you explore the American Swedish Institute:

Historic Mansion: The ASI is housed in the historic Turnblad Mansion, a beautiful and well-preserved example of the Châteauesque architectural style. The mansion itself is a work of art, with its intricate woodwork, stained glass, and period furnishings.

Art and Exhibitions: The institute hosts a range of rotating exhibitions that explore various aspects of Swedish and Swedish-American culture, history, and contemporary art. These exhibitions often feature works by Swedish and Nordic artists.

Permanent Collection: The ASI has a permanent collection that includes a diverse range of items, from traditional Swedish folk art and textiles to contemporary Swedish design. The collection reflects the rich cultural heritage of Sweden and the influence of Swedish immigrants in the United States.

Cultural Events: The institute hosts a variety of cultural events and programs throughout the year. These may include concerts, lectures, workshops, craft demonstrations, and traditional Swedish celebrations like the Midsommar Festival and St. Lucia Celebration.

Gardens: The ASI features beautiful outdoor gardens and courtyards that are a peaceful oasis in the heart of the city. Visitors can explore the gardens, which often feature sculptures and artistic installations.

Family-Friendly Activities: The institute offers family-friendly programs and activities, making it an engaging destination for visitors of all ages. Interactive exhibits and hands-on experiences are designed to educate and entertain.

Café and Museum Store: The ASI has an on-site café where you can enjoy Swedish-inspired cuisine and pastries. There's also a museum store where you can find Nordic-inspired gifts, books, and specialty food items.

Language and Culture Programs: The institute offers language classes and cultural programs for those interested in learning more about the Swedish language and culture.

Education and Outreach: The ASI is dedicated to education and outreach, partnering with schools and community organizations to promote cross-cultural understanding and appreciation of Swedish heritage.

Membership: Becoming a member of the American Swedish Institute often provides benefits such as free admission, discounts on programs and events, and exclusive access to members-only events.

Accessibility: The ASI strives to be accessible to all visitors, providing services such as wheelchair accessibility and assistive listening devices.

Whether you have Swedish heritage or simply an interest in Nordic culture, the American Swedish Institute offers a unique opportunity to explore the rich history, art, and traditions of Sweden. It's a welcoming and vibrant cultural center that fosters cross-cultural connections and appreciation for Swedish contributions to American society.

8. Visit the Mill City Museum.

The Mill City Museum is a fascinating and engaging cultural institution located in Minneapolis, Minnesota. It tells the story of the city's milling history and its pivotal role in the flour milling industry. Here's what you can expect when you visit the Mill City Museum:

Historical Significance: The Mill City Museum is situated on the historic ruins of the Washburn "A" Mill, which was once the largest and most advanced flour mill in the world. It played a crucial role in Minneapolis's development as the "Flour Milling Capital of the World."

Interactive Exhibits: The museum features interactive exhibits that take visitors on a journey through time. You'll learn about the history of flour milling in Minneapolis, the impact of the industry on the city's growth, and the stories of the people who worked in the mills.

Flour Tower: One of the highlights of the museum is the Flour Tower, an immersive multimedia experience that simulates the process of flour milling. Visitors ride an elevator to the top of the tower while watching videos and learning about the milling process. It provides a unique perspective on the inner workings of a flour mill.

Historic Milling Equipment: The museum displays historic milling equipment, including massive millstones and machinery from the Washburn "A" Mill. You can see these artifacts up close and learn how they operated.

Ruin Courtyard: The outdoor Ruin Courtyard features the preserved ruins of the Washburn "A" Mill, providing a glimpse into the past. It's a picturesque setting with views of the Mississippi River and the Stone Arch Bridge.

Baking Lab: The museum often hosts demonstrations and hands-on activities in its Baking Lab, where you can learn about the science of baking and even sample freshly baked goods.

Education and Programs: The Mill City Museum offers educational programs for visitors of all ages, including school groups. There are guided tours, workshops, and special events that explore various aspects of milling history and the development of Minneapolis.

Family-Friendly: The museum is family-friendly and provides engaging exhibits and activities for children, making it an educational and enjoyable destination for families.

Riverfront Location: The museum is located along the scenic Mississippi River, near the historic Stone Arch Bridge and Mill Ruins Park. The riverfront location offers picturesque views and opportunities for leisurely walks and picnics.

Museum Store: The museum has a store where you can purchase books, gifts, and souvenirs related to milling history and Minneapolis.

Membership: Becoming a member of the Mill City Museum often provides benefits such as free admission, discounts on programs and events, and exclusive access to members-only activities.

Visiting the Mill City Museum is not only a journey into Minneapolis's industrial past but also an opportunity to appreciate the city's resilience, innovation, and cultural heritage. It's a must-visit destination for history enthusiasts, families, and anyone interested in understanding the impact of milling on the development of Minneapolis.

9.Experience local theater at the Mixed Blood Theatre.

The Mixed Blood Theatre is a dynamic and culturally diverse theater company located in Minneapolis, Minnesota, known for its commitment to presenting thought-provoking and socially relevant theater productions. Here's what you can expect when you experience local theater at the Mixed Blood Theatre:

Mission and Values: Mixed Blood Theatre is dedicated to promoting social change and addressing issues of diversity, equity, and inclusion through the performing arts. The theater's productions often explore themes related to race, identity, immigration, and social justice.

Diverse Productions: The theater company produces a wide range of plays, from classic works to contemporary pieces, and even original productions. Many of these productions feature diverse casts and artistic teams, reflecting a commitment to representing a variety of voices and perspectives.

Accessible Theater: Mixed Blood Theatre strives to make theater accessible to all audiences. It offers a unique system of admission that includes free shows for those who may not be able to afford traditional theater tickets, ensuring that theater is available to everyone in the community.

Mainstage Productions: The theater's mainstage productions are held in its historic firehouse location in the Cedar-Riverside neighborhood of Minneapolis. These productions often tackle complex and relevant social issues, encouraging critical thinking and dialogue.

Radical Hospitality: The theater's "Radical Hospitality" initiative provides no-cost admission to many performances, allowing audiences of diverse backgrounds and financial means to attend and engage with the productions.

Interactive Performances: Some productions at Mixed Blood Theatre involve interactive elements, encouraging audience participation and immersion in the story.

Community Engagement: The theater actively engages with the local community through outreach programs, partnerships with schools, and workshops that provide educational opportunities for students and aspiring artists.

Youth Programming: Mixed Blood Theatre offers youth programs and opportunities for young actors and artists to develop their skills and gain experience in the performing arts.

Membership and Support: Becoming a member or donor of Mixed Blood Theatre often provides opportunities for exclusive access, discounts, and invitations to special events.

Collaborative Approach: The theater frequently collaborates with local artists, writers, and organizations to create new works and develop innovative approaches to storytelling.

Relevant and Timely: The productions at Mixed Blood Theatre are often grounded in current events and contemporary issues, sparking meaningful conversations and reflections among audience members.

Experiencing local theater at Mixed Blood Theatre is not just about attending a performance; it's about engaging with thought-provoking art that challenges perceptions, fosters empathy, and encourages dialogue about the pressing social issues of our time. It's a unique and enriching cultural experience that reflects the theater's dedication to inclusivity and community engagement.

10.Explore the Minneapolis Sculpture Garden.

The Minneapolis Sculpture Garden is a beloved outdoor art space and cultural destination located in Minneapolis, Minnesota. It is known for its impressive collection of sculptures, beautifully landscaped gardens, and its iconic centerpiece, the "Spoonbridge and Cherry" sculpture. Here's what you can expect when you explore the Minneapolis Sculpture Garden:

Outdoor Art Gallery: The Minneapolis Sculpture Garden is one of the largest urban sculpture gardens in the country, spanning 11 acres of land. It features over 40 permanent sculptures created by both local and internationally renowned artists. The sculptures represent a wide range of styles, materials, and artistic concepts, making it a diverse and visually stimulating outdoor art gallery.

Spoonbridge and Cherry: The "Spoonbridge and Cherry" sculpture, created by Claes Oldenburg and Coosje van Bruggen, is the most iconic and recognizable artwork in the garden. This whimsical sculpture consists of a giant spoon with a cherry perched on its tip, symbolizing Minneapolis's connection to food and the Mississippi River.

Interactive Art: Many of the sculptures in the garden invite interaction and exploration. Visitors are encouraged to walk around, touch, and even climb on certain pieces, creating a participatory and engaging experience.

Beautiful Landscaping: The garden is beautifully landscaped with a combination of native and ornamental plants, reflecting the changing seasons and providing a tranquil setting for both art and nature enthusiasts.

Paved Pathways: The garden features well-maintained paved pathways that make it accessible to visitors of all ages and abilities. These pathways guide you through the garden, allowing you to discover sculptures at your own pace.

Free Admission: The Minneapolis Sculpture Garden is open to the public and offers free admission, making it an accessible and affordable destination for art and nature lovers.

Cultural Events: The garden hosts a variety of cultural events throughout the year, including outdoor concerts, film screenings, yoga classes, and special exhibitions. These events add vibrancy and cultural richness to the space.

Accessibility: The garden is designed to be accessible to all visitors, with accommodations for individuals with disabilities, including wheelchair-accessible pathways and restrooms.

Picnic Areas: There are designated picnic areas in the garden where you can enjoy a meal or a snack while surrounded by art and nature.

Photography: The Minneapolis Sculpture Garden is a popular spot for photography, whether you're a professional photographer or just looking to capture memories of your visit.

Educational Opportunities: The garden offers educational programs and guided tours for school groups and visitors interested in learning more about the sculptures and the artists behind them.

Membership and Support: Becoming a member or donor of the Walker Art Center, which oversees the garden, often provides benefits such as exclusive access to events and discounts on programs.

The Minneapolis Sculpture Garden is a serene and inspiring space where art and nature converge, offering a delightful and enriching experience for residents and visitors alike. Whether you're a seasoned art enthusiast or simply looking for a peaceful outdoor setting, the garden provides a unique blend of artistic and natural beauty.

11.Bike or walk around Lake Calhoun (Bde Maka Ska).

Biking or walking around Lake Calhoun, also known as Bde Maka Ska, is a popular outdoor activity in Minneapolis, Minnesota, offering a scenic and recreational experience in the heart of the city. Here's what you can expect when you explore this beautiful urban lake:

Scenic Beauty: Lake Calhoun/Bde Maka Ska is one of the most picturesque spots in Minneapolis. Its clear waters are surrounded by lush greenery, including trees, parks, and beaches. The lake's natural beauty is especially stunning during the changing seasons.

Walking Path: The lake features a 3.2-mile paved walking and biking path that encircles its shoreline. This path is perfect for leisurely strolls, brisk walks, or invigorating runs. It's also a great place for cyclists, and many people bring their bikes to enjoy a ride around the lake.

Beaches: There are several beaches along the lake, such as Thomas Beach and 32nd Street Beach, where you can relax, swim, or sunbathe during the summer months. The beaches offer a refreshing escape from the city's hustle and bustle.

Water Activities: Lake Calhoun/Bde Maka Ska is a popular spot for water activities like paddleboarding, kayaking, and canoeing. You can bring your own equipment or rent from nearby vendors.

Wildlife Viewing: The lake and its surrounding parkland are home to a variety of wildlife, including waterfowl, songbirds, and occasionally even bald eagles. Birdwatching is a rewarding activity here.

Picnicking: The lake is dotted with picnic areas, making it a great spot for a picnic lunch or dinner. You can enjoy a meal with a view of the water and the Minneapolis skyline in the distance.

Rest Stops: Along the path, you'll find benches, rest areas, and water fountains, providing opportunities to take a break and soak in the scenery.

Dog-Friendly: Lake Calhoun/Bde Maka Ska is a dog-friendly destination. Many people bring their dogs for walks or runs, and there's a designated off-leash dog park nearby for even more canine fun.

Fitness Stations: The walking path also features fitness stations where you can incorporate bodyweight exercises into your walk or run.

Seasonal Changes: The lake offers a different experience in each season. In the winter, you can enjoy ice skating and cross-country skiing on the frozen lake, while spring and fall offer mild weather and vibrant foliage.

Accessibility: The path around the lake is accessible to people of all abilities, making it inclusive for everyone to enjoy.

Parking and Amenities: There are parking lots and facilities, including restrooms, located around the lake for your convenience.

Biking or walking around Lake Calhoun/Bde Maka Ska is a peaceful and refreshing way to connect with nature, enjoy outdoor exercise, and appreciate the natural beauty that Minneapolis has to offer. Whether you're a local looking for a regular escape or a visitor exploring the city, this urban oasis is a must-visit destination.

12.Go for a hike in Minnehaha Regional Park.

Hiking in Minnehaha Regional Park is a delightful outdoor adventure that allows you to explore scenic landscapes, dramatic waterfalls, and natural beauty in the heart of Minneapolis, Minnesota. Here's what you can expect when you go for a hike in Minnehaha Regional Park:

Minnehaha Falls: The park is best known for its stunning 53-foot Minnehaha Falls, a breathtaking natural waterfall that cascades over limestone cliffs. The falls are the centerpiece of the park and a must-see attraction. You can approach the falls via paved walkways for a close-up view, and there are multiple viewing platforms to capture the beauty of the falls.

Hiking Trails: The park offers several hiking trails that wind through wooded areas, along the creek, and up and down hills. The trails vary in length and difficulty, making it suitable for hikers of all skill levels. Whether you prefer a leisurely stroll or a more challenging hike, you'll find a trail that suits your preferences.

Scenic Overlooks: Along the trails, you'll encounter scenic overlooks that provide panoramic views of the creek, gorge, and the surrounding natural landscape. These overlooks offer excellent photo opportunities and moments of tranquility.

Creek Walks: The hiking trails follow Minnehaha Creek, allowing you to enjoy the soothing sounds of flowing water and the sight of the creek meandering through the forested landscape.

Bridge Crossings: The park features picturesque footbridges that span the creek, adding to the charm of your hike and providing scenic spots for contemplation.

Flora and Fauna: Minnehaha Regional Park is home to a variety of native plant species and wildlife. Keep an eye out for birds, squirrels, and other creatures that inhabit the area.

Picnic Areas: The park has designated picnic areas where you can take a break, enjoy a meal, or have a picnic with friends and family. It's a great way to combine outdoor dining with your hike.

Cultural Attractions: In addition to its natural beauty, the park is home to historic attractions such as the John H. Stevens House and Minnehaha Depot, providing insights into the area's history.

Visitor Center: The park's visitor center offers information, maps, and exhibits that can enhance your understanding of the park's natural and cultural features.

Photography: Minnehaha Regional Park is a popular spot for photography, with opportunities to capture the beauty of the falls, the creek, and the surrounding foliage throughout the seasons.

Accessibility: The park is designed to be accessible to people of all abilities, with designated accessible trails and facilities.

Events and Activities: The park hosts events and activities throughout the year, including nature programs, concerts, and festivals, providing additional opportunities for enjoyment and exploration.

Hiking in Minnehaha Regional Park is a wonderful way to escape the city's hustle and bustle, connect with nature, and appreciate the beauty of the outdoors. Whether you're a nature enthusiast, a history buff, or simply seeking a peaceful and scenic hike, Minnehaha Regional Park offers a memorable and rejuvenating experience.

13.Canoe or kayak on the Chain of Lakes.

Canoeing or kayaking on the Chain of Lakes in Minneapolis, Minnesota, is a delightful outdoor activity that allows you to enjoy the natural beauty of the interconnected lakes while exploring the urban wilderness. Here's what you can expect when you paddle on the Chain of Lakes:

Interconnected Lakes: The Chain of Lakes includes several beautiful lakes, including Lake Calhoun (Bde Maka Ska), Lake Harriet, Lake Isles, Cedar Lake, and Brownie Lake. These lakes are interconnected by scenic waterways, giving you the opportunity to explore multiple bodies of water in a single outing.

Watercraft Rentals: You can rent canoes, kayaks, paddleboards, and other watercraft from rental facilities located around the lakes. Rentals are available during the warm-weather months, typically from spring to early fall.

Scenic Views: Paddling on the Chain of Lakes offers stunning views of the Minneapolis skyline, lush parkland, wooded shores, and the surrounding urban and natural landscapes. You'll encounter picturesque vistas and wildlife along the way.

Tranquil Experience: Despite being located in the heart of the city, the lakes provide a tranquil and peaceful environment for paddlers. It's a wonderful way to escape the hustle and bustle of urban life and connect with nature.

Wildlife Viewing: The lakes are home to various wildlife species, including waterfowl, birds, turtles, and occasionally even eagles. Birdwatching is a popular activity while paddling.

Fishing: Fishing is allowed on some of the lakes, and you can catch species like bass, pike, and sunfish. Be sure to check local regulations and obtain any necessary permits.

Picnicking: Many areas around the lakes have designated picnic spots where you can enjoy a meal or a snack. Some rental facilities even offer picnic equipment with your rental.

Swimming: Some of the lakes have designated swimming areas if you wish to take a refreshing dip during your paddling adventure.

Fitness and Relaxation: Paddling on the lakes provides both a recreational workout and a relaxing experience. Whether you prefer a leisurely paddle or a more vigorous workout, the Chain of Lakes offers options for all levels of paddlers.

Events and Activities: The Chain of Lakes often hosts events and activities, such as paddle races, paddleboard yoga classes, and environmental education programs.

Safety: It's important to follow safety guidelines while paddling, including wearing life jackets and being aware of local water conditions and regulations.

Sunset Paddles: Sunset paddles on the Chain of Lakes offer a magical experience as you watch the sun dip below the horizon, casting a warm glow over the water.

Paddling on the Chain of Lakes is a memorable and scenic way to experience the natural beauty of Minneapolis while engaging in a relaxing and recreational outdoor activity. Whether you're a seasoned paddler or a novice looking for a new adventure, the Chain of Lakes provides a unique urban oasis for water enthusiasts.

14.Play golf at one of the city's golf courses.

Playing golf at one of Minneapolis's golf courses is a popular outdoor recreational activity for both residents and visitors. The city offers several golf courses that cater to a range of skill levels and preferences. Here's what you can expect when you play golf at one of Minneapolis's golf courses:

Travel to Minneapolis Minnesota

Scenic Courses: Minneapolis's golf courses are known for their scenic beauty, often set amidst lush greenery, rolling hills, and natural landscapes. Many of them provide a peaceful escape from the city's urban hustle and bustle.

Variety of Courses: Minneapolis boasts a variety of golf courses, including public, municipal, and private clubs. You can choose from courses that challenge your skills or opt for more casual rounds, depending on your experience level and preferences.

City Views: Some golf courses offer panoramic views of the Minneapolis skyline, creating a unique golfing experience that combines the urban and natural landscapes.

Well-Maintained Fairways: The courses are typically well-maintained with manicured fairways, greens, and bunkers, ensuring an enjoyable and challenging golfing experience.

Golf Lessons: If you're a beginner or looking to improve your game, many courses offer golf lessons and clinics taught by experienced golf professionals.

Pro Shops: Golf courses often have pro shops where you can purchase golf equipment, clothing, and accessories. You can also rent golf clubs and carts if needed.

Clubhouses and Dining: Clubhouses at golf courses often provide dining options, including restaurants or snack bars, where you can enjoy a meal or refreshments before or after your round.

Tournaments and Events: Many golf courses host tournaments, charity events, and golf outings, providing opportunities for friendly competition and community engagement.

Membership Options: Some golf courses offer membership options, providing regular golfers with benefits such as tee time reservations, discounts, and exclusive access to member-only events.

Accessibility: Most golf courses are accessible to golfers of all abilities, with tees at various levels to accommodate different skill levels.

Seasonal Play: Golf courses are typically open seasonally, from spring to fall, depending on weather conditions. Be sure to check course availability and book tee times in advance.

Golf Etiquette: As with any golf course, it's essential to observe proper golf etiquette, such as repairing divots, replacing ball marks, and maintaining a reasonable pace of play.

Some of the well-known golf courses in Minneapolis include Theodore Wirth Golf Course, Hiawatha Golf Club, and Columbia Golf Course, among others. Whether you're an avid golfer or looking to try golf for the first time, playing golf at one of Minneapolis's golf courses offers a enjoyable and leisurely way to spend time outdoors while indulging in your love for the sport.

15. Visit the Eloise Butler Wildflower Garden and Bird Sanctuary.

Visiting the Eloise Butler Wildflower Garden and Bird Sanctuary is a serene and educational experience that allows you to immerse yourself in the beauty of native wildflowers and observe various bird species in a natural setting. Here's what you can expect when you explore this unique natural sanctuary in Minneapolis, Minnesota:

Native Wildflowers: The Eloise Butler Wildflower Garden is renowned for its extensive collection of native wildflowers. You can wander along the well-maintained paths and observe a stunning array of wildflower species, including trilliums, lady's slippers, violets, and more. The garden's design allows for seasonal blooms, so different times of the year offer varying displays of colorful and fragrant flowers.

Bird Watching: The sanctuary is a birdwatcher's paradise, providing opportunities to spot a diverse range of bird species. You can bring your binoculars and camera to capture sightings of local and migratory birds. Commonly seen birds include warblers, sparrows, woodpeckers, and songbirds.

Natural Habitat: Eloise Butler Wildflower Garden and Bird Sanctuary is designed to replicate the natural habitat of Minnesota, with its mix of woodlands, wetlands, prairies, and open water. This diversity of ecosystems creates a haven for both plant and animal life.

Educational Experience: The garden is dedicated to environmental education and conservation. You'll find informative signage and interpretive displays that provide insights into the flora, fauna, and ecology of the area.

Tranquil Setting: The sanctuary offers a tranquil and peaceful environment, making it an ideal place for nature enthusiasts, photographers, or anyone seeking a break from the hustle and bustle of city life.

Seasonal Changes: The garden transforms throughout the seasons, offering different experiences in spring, summer, fall, and even winter. Spring and summer bring lush blooms, while fall showcases vibrant foliage, and winter offers a quieter, snow-covered landscape.

Accessibility: The paths in the garden are designed to be accessible to visitors of all abilities, ensuring that everyone can enjoy the natural beauty of the sanctuary.

Events and Programs: Eloise Butler Wildflower Garden and Bird Sanctuary often hosts educational programs, guided hikes, and special events that allow you to deepen your understanding of the local flora and fauna.

Picnic Areas: There are designated picnic areas where you can relax, enjoy a meal, or simply savor the sights and sounds of nature.

Membership and Support: Becoming a member or donor of the Friends of the Eloise Butler Wildflower Garden and Bird Sanctuary can provide benefits such as exclusive access to events and opportunities to support the preservation of this natural gem.

Visiting the Eloise Butler Wildflower Garden and Bird Sanctuary is a way to reconnect with nature, learn about native flora and fauna, and appreciate the importance of preserving natural habitats. Whether you're a botany enthusiast, a bird lover, or simply seeking a peaceful natural retreat, this sanctuary offers a serene and educational experience in the heart of Minneapolis.

16. Take a Segway tour along the riverfront.

Taking a Segway tour along the riverfront in Minneapolis is a fun and unique way to explore the city's scenic landscapes, historic sites, and vibrant culture.

Here's what you can expect when you embark on a Segway tour along the riverfront:

Scenic River Views: As you glide along the riverfront on your Segway, you'll enjoy breathtaking views of the Mississippi River and the picturesque Stone Arch Bridge. This iconic bridge is a symbol of Minneapolis and offers a perfect backdrop for memorable photos.

Historical Sites: Many Segway tours along the riverfront include stops at historical sites and landmarks. For example, you might visit the Mill Ruins Park, where you can learn about Minneapolis's milling history and see the preserved ruins of the Washburn "A" Mill. The area is rich in history and offers a glimpse into the city's industrial past.

Local Guides: Knowledgeable and experienced local guides often lead Segway tours, providing interesting commentary and insights into the city's history, culture, and architecture. They can answer questions, share fun facts, and make the tour informative and engaging.

Cultural Districts: Some Segway tours explore nearby cultural districts, such as the historic St. Anthony Main district, known for its charming cobblestone streets, theaters, and dining options. It's a great way to experience the city's vibrant cultural scene.

Accessible for All: Segway tours are designed to be accessible to people of various fitness levels and abilities. Most tour operators provide training and practice sessions to ensure everyone feels comfortable and safe riding a Segway.

Small Group Experience: Segway tours often have small group sizes, creating an intimate and personalized experience. This allows for more interaction with the guide and fellow participants.

Safety First: Safety is a priority on Segway tours. Participants are typically provided with helmets and receive thorough safety instructions before the tour begins.

Diverse Tour Options: Tour operators offer various tour options, including daytime and evening tours, themed tours (e.g., history, architecture, or ghost tours), and tours of different durations. You can choose the one that best suits your interests and schedule.

Fun and Memorable: Riding a Segway is a unique and exhilarating experience, making the tour not only informative but also a lot of fun. It's an excellent way to create lasting memories of your visit to Minneapolis.

Age Restrictions: While Segway tours are accessible for many age groups, there may be age and weight restrictions for safety reasons. Be sure to check with the tour operator for specific requirements.

Taking a Segway tour along the riverfront in Minneapolis allows you to cover a significant area while enjoying the scenic beauty and cultural richness of the city. Whether you're a local looking to explore your city from a new perspective or a visitor seeking an exciting way to discover Minneapolis, a Segway tour offers a unique and memorable adventure.

17.Go ice skating at The Depot's indoor rink.

Ice skating at The Depot's indoor rink in Minneapolis is a delightful winter activity that offers a fun and family-friendly experience. Here's what you can expect when you go ice skating at The Depot:

Indoor Ice Rink: The Depot's ice rink is located indoors, which means you can enjoy ice skating in a climate-controlled environment. This is especially appealing during the winter months when outdoor temperatures can be quite cold.

Open to All Skill Levels: The rink is open to skaters of all ages and skill levels, making it a great place for both beginners and experienced skaters to enjoy some time on the ice.

Rental Equipment: If you don't have your own ice skates, The Depot offers rental equipment, including ice skates, helmets, and lockers for your belongings. This makes it convenient for visitors who may not have their own gear.

Family-Friendly Atmosphere: The Depot's indoor ice rink is known for its family-friendly atmosphere. It's a popular destination for families, friends, and individuals looking for a fun and recreational outing.

Skating Sessions: The rink typically offers scheduled skating sessions throughout the day. These sessions may include open skate, family skate, and themed events. Be sure to check the schedule for specific times and skate types.

Skate Aids: Some indoor ice rinks, including The Depot, offer skate aids like penguin or snowman-shaped devices that young or inexperienced skaters can use for balance and support.

Ice Skating Lessons: If you're a beginner or looking to improve your skating skills, The Depot often provides ice skating lessons taught by experienced instructors. These lessons are a great way to build confidence on the ice.

Group Events: The Depot's ice rink can also be reserved for group events, such as birthday parties, corporate outings, and private gatherings. It's a fun and unique setting for special occasions.

Dining Options: The Depot may have dining options on-site, allowing you to enjoy a meal or refreshments before or after your skating session.

Seasonal Activity: Ice skating at The Depot is typically a seasonal activity, with the rink open during the winter months. Be sure to check the rink's operating hours and availability, especially if you plan to visit outside of the winter season.

Safety Measures: Indoor ice rinks usually have safety measures in place, including well-maintained ice surfaces and staff trained in first aid. Be sure to follow any posted rules and guidelines for a safe and enjoyable skating experience.

Ice skating at The Depot's indoor rink is a classic winter activity that brings joy and excitement to individuals and families alike. Whether you're looking to practice your skating skills, spend quality time with loved ones, or simply enjoy the thrill of gliding on ice, The Depot provides a welcoming and accessible venue for ice skating enthusiasts.

18.Explore the Como Park Zoo and Conservatory in nearby St. Paul.

Exploring the Como Park Zoo and Conservatory in nearby St. Paul is a fantastic experience that allows you to immerse yourself in the beauty of botanical gardens and observe a diverse array of animals. Here's what you can expect when you visit Como Park Zoo and Conservatory:

Botanical Gardens: The Como Park Conservatory is renowned for its stunning botanical gardens. You can wander through a variety of lush and beautifully landscaped gardens, each with its own unique theme and collection of plants. Some of the gardens you may encounter include the Sunken Garden, Tropical Encounters, and the Bonsai Collection.

Year-Round Beauty: The conservatory is open year-round, providing a welcome escape from the cold Minnesota winters. Inside, you'll find a warm and tropical oasis where you can enjoy the vibrant colors and fragrant blooms, regardless of the season.

Animal Encounters: Como Park Zoo is home to a diverse range of animals from around the world. You can observe animals such as lions, tigers, giraffes, polar bears, penguins, primates, and more. The zoo's commitment to animal welfare and conservation is evident in its well-designed habitats.

Educational Experiences: Como Park offers educational experiences for visitors of all ages. You'll find informative signage, interactive exhibits, and opportunities to learn about animal behavior, conservation efforts, and the importance of biodiversity.

Conservation Initiatives: The zoo is actively involved in conservation initiatives, and you can learn about their efforts to protect endangered species and their natural habitats. Supporting conservation is a central mission of Como Park.

Family-Friendly: Como Park is family-friendly and offers engaging activities for children. The zoo often hosts special events, animal encounters, and interactive exhibits that cater to young visitors.

Accessibility: The facilities at Como Park are designed to be accessible to people of all abilities, ensuring that everyone can enjoy the gardens and animal exhibits.

Picnic Areas: There are designated picnic areas where you can enjoy a meal or a snack surrounded by the beauty of the gardens and the sounds of nature.

Visitor Center: The park has a visitor center with information, maps, and resources to enhance your visit. You can also find gift shops where you can purchase souvenirs and gifts related to the conservatory and zoo.

Membership and Support: Becoming a member or donor of Como Friends, the nonprofit organization that supports Como Park, can provide benefits such as exclusive access to events, discounts, and the satisfaction of supporting conservation and education efforts.

Events and Programs: Como Park often hosts special events, seasonal celebrations, and educational programs that add to the richness of your visit. Be sure to check their event calendar for upcoming activities.

Visiting Como Park Zoo and Conservatory is a multi-sensory experience that combines the beauty of nature with the wonder of wildlife. Whether you're a plant enthusiast, an animal lover, or simply seeking a tranquil and educational outing, Como Park offers a memorable and enriching day trip in the Twin Cities area.

19.Enjoy a day of fishing on the Mississippi River.

Enjoying a day of fishing on the Mississippi River in the Minneapolis area is a fantastic way to connect with nature, relax, and potentially catch a variety of fish species. Here's what you can expect when you plan a day of fishing on the Mississippi River:

Fishing Opportunities: The Mississippi River offers diverse fishing opportunities, with the chance to catch a variety of fish species. Common catches in the area may include bass, walleye, northern pike, catfish, panfish, and more. The river's waters are known for their abundance of fish, making it a popular destination for anglers.

Scenic Beauty: Fishing on the Mississippi River allows you to enjoy the scenic beauty of the waterway, which winds through picturesque landscapes, including lush forests, serene backwaters, and rocky shorelines. It's a chance to appreciate the natural beauty of the area while pursuing your favorite pastime.

Public Access Points: There are numerous public access points along the Mississippi River, where you can launch your boat, cast from the shore, or fish from a pier. These access points are well-maintained and provide convenient entry to the river.

Boating Options: If you have access to a boat or kayak, you can explore different sections of the river, seeking out your preferred fishing spots. Alternatively, some anglers prefer fishing from the riverbanks or designated fishing piers.

Fishing Licenses: Be sure to obtain the necessary fishing licenses and permits required for fishing in Minnesota waters. These can typically be purchased online or at local bait shops.

Tackle and Gear: Bring along your fishing tackle, rods, reels, bait, and other gear. You can also find bait shops in the area if you need to stock up on live bait or lures.

Regulations: Familiarize yourself with local fishing regulations, including size limits, catch limits, and any special rules for the section of the river you plan to fish in. This helps ensure that you're fishing responsibly and in compliance with conservation efforts.

Wildlife Observation: While fishing, take the opportunity to observe the wildlife along the river. You might spot waterfowl, birds of prey, and other wildlife in their natural habitat.

Safety: Safety is paramount when fishing on the Mississippi River. Be aware of the water conditions, wear appropriate safety gear, and follow best practices for water safety.

Catch and Release: Some anglers practice catch and release, which helps conserve fish populations and maintain a healthy ecosystem. If you choose to release fish, handle them gently and release them back into the water promptly.

Picnic and Relaxation: Many fishing spots along the river have picnic areas or scenic overlooks where you can relax, enjoy a meal, or simply savor the tranquility of the river.

Fishing on the Mississippi River offers a serene and rewarding experience for both novice and experienced anglers. Whether you're seeking a peaceful day of fishing or hoping to reel in a big catch, the river's diverse fishing opportunities make it a great destination for those who love the sport.

20.Go cross-country skiing in Theodore Wirth Regional Park.

Cross-country skiing in Theodore Wirth Regional Park is a wonderful way to embrace winter, get some exercise, and explore the natural beauty of this urban park in Minneapolis, Minnesota. Here's what you can expect when you go cross-country skiing in Theodore Wirth Regional Park:

Trails for All Skill Levels: Theodore Wirth Regional Park offers a network of cross-country skiing trails that cater to skiers of all skill levels. Whether you're a beginner or an experienced skier, you can find trails suited to your abilities.

Trail Variety: The park features a variety of trails, including classic skiing trails and skate skiing trails. The classic style involves a gliding motion, while skate skiing resembles the motion of ice skating. You can choose the technique that best suits your preferences.

Groomed Trails: Many of the skiing trails in Theodore Wirth Regional Park are groomed regularly to provide smooth and well-maintained surfaces. Grooming ensures a more enjoyable skiing experience and helps with traction and control.

Rental Equipment: If you don't have your own cross-country skiing equipment, you can often rent skis, poles, and boots from rental facilities within the park or nearby shops. Rental equipment is typically available for both classic and skate skiing styles.

Lessons and Programs: The park sometimes offers cross-country skiing lessons and programs for skiers of all ages and abilities. These programs are a great way to improve your skills or try cross-country skiing for the first time.

Scenic Beauty: Skiing in Theodore Wirth Regional Park allows you to enjoy the park's natural beauty in a winter setting. You'll ski through snow-covered forests, open fields, and alongside frozen lakes, providing picturesque views and opportunities for wildlife sightings.

Winter Wildlife: Keep an eye out for winter wildlife such as deer, birds, and other animals that are active during the colder months. Skiing in a natural setting can lead to memorable wildlife encounters.

Snowshoeing: Some skiers enjoy combining their cross-country skiing with snowshoeing. Theodore Wirth Regional Park offers snowshoeing trails as well, allowing you to explore on foot if you wish.

Trail Maps: The park typically provides trail maps and signage to help you navigate the ski trails and plan your route.

Warm-Up Facilities: Some parks have warm-up facilities with heated shelters, restrooms, and places to take a break and warm up during your ski outing.

Winter Events: Theodore Wirth Regional Park often hosts winter events and races, providing opportunities to participate in or spectate cross-country skiing competitions and other winter activities.

Winter Wonderland: Skiing in a snow-covered landscape creates a winter wonderland ambiance that's perfect for outdoor enthusiasts and those looking to embrace the magic of winter.

Cross-country skiing in Theodore Wirth Regional Park offers a peaceful and invigorating way to enjoy the outdoors during the winter season. Whether you're a seasoned skier or a newcomer to the sport, the park's trails and amenities provide an ideal setting for a day of cross-country skiing in the heart of Minneapolis.

21.Try a Juicy Lucy burger at Matt's Bar.

Trying a Juicy Lucy burger at Matt's Bar is a quintessential Minneapolis dining experience that offers a unique and delicious take on the classic hamburger. Here's what you can expect when you indulge in a Juicy Lucy burger at Matt's Bar:

Juicy Lucy Definition: A Juicy Lucy, also spelled Jucy Lucy, is a type of cheeseburger that is known for its juicy, molten cheese center. The twist is that the cheese is sealed inside the meat patty, creating a burst of hot, gooey cheese when you bite into the burger.

Cheese Filling: At Matt's Bar, the Juicy Lucy consists of two beef patties with a slice of American cheese placed between them. The patties are pressed together at the edges to seal the cheese inside. As the burger cooks on the grill, the cheese melts, resulting in a mouthwatering, cheesy explosion when you take a bite.

Classic Accompaniments: Typically, a Juicy Lucy burger is served on a bun with classic toppings such as lettuce, tomato, pickles, and onions. You can also add condiments like ketchup and mustard to suit your taste.

Side Choices: Matt's Bar typically offers a variety of side dishes to complement your burger, including french fries, onion rings, and coleslaw.

Local Favorite: Matt's Bar is a local institution in Minneapolis, and it's often credited with inventing the Juicy Lucy burger. The restaurant has a cozy and unassuming atmosphere, making it a beloved spot for locals and visitors alike.

Casual Dining: Matt's Bar is a casual dining establishment, so you can expect a laid-back and welcoming atmosphere. It's a place where you can enjoy a delicious burger without the need for formal attire.

Local Flavor: Dining at Matt's Bar allows you to savor a unique Minneapolis culinary tradition. The Juicy Lucy has become an iconic local dish, and trying one at its place of origin is a must for food enthusiasts and burger lovers.

Savoring the Experience: Eating a Juicy Lucy requires a bit of caution, as the hot cheese inside can be molten. It's a messy, flavorful, and enjoyable experience that's all part of the fun.

Local Lore: The history and rivalry surrounding the Juicy Lucy are part of Minneapolis lore. Matt's Bar and other local spots like the 5-8 Club have their own versions of the Juicy Lucy, and some residents passionately debate which one is the best.

Cash-Only: As a tip, be prepared to pay with cash at Matt's Bar, as it typically does not accept credit cards.

Trying a Juicy Lucy burger at Matt's Bar is not only about savoring a delicious and indulgent meal but also about immersing yourself in a local culinary tradition that has captured the hearts and taste buds of Minneapolis residents for generations. It's a flavorful experience that adds a dash of regional charm to your visit to the city.

22.Sample Scandinavian cuisine at Fika.

Sampling Scandinavian cuisine at Fika is a delightful culinary experience that offers a taste of the Nordic flavors and traditions in the heart of Minneapolis. Here's what you can expect when you dine at Fika:

Nordic Flavors: Fika, which means "coffee break" in Swedish, specializes in offering a menu that celebrates the flavors of Scandinavia. You can expect dishes that highlight fresh, locally sourced ingredients prepared with a Nordic twist.

Menu Variety: The menu at Fika typically features a range of Scandinavian-inspired dishes, including seafood, meat, and vegetarian options. Some popular dishes you might encounter include gravlax (cured salmon), Swedish meatballs, herring, open-faced sandwiches, and various types of pickled vegetables.

Smorgasbord: Fika occasionally offers a smorgasbord, a traditional Swedish buffet-style meal that allows you to sample a wide variety of dishes. Smorgasbords often include an array of herring, cured fish, salads, and desserts.

Bakery Treats: Scandinavian cuisine is known for its baked goods and pastries. At Fika, you can indulge in sweet treats like cardamom buns, almond cakes, and Swedish princess cake, a layer cake covered in marzipan.

Coffee and Beverages: Fika takes its coffee seriously. You can pair your meal with a cup of high-quality coffee, or try Scandinavian beverages like aquavit, a traditional Nordic spirit often infused with herbs and spices.

Seasonal Ingredients: The menu at Fika often changes with the seasons, allowing you to savor dishes made from the freshest, seasonal ingredients available.

Cozy Atmosphere: Fika typically offers a cozy and inviting atmosphere with Scandinavian-inspired decor. It's a place where you can enjoy a leisurely meal with friends, family, or a special someone.

Nordic Traditions: Dining at Fika allows you to experience some of the culinary traditions and flavors of Sweden and other Scandinavian countries. The restaurant strives to capture the essence of Nordic cuisine.

Culinary Events: Fika occasionally hosts culinary events and themed dinners that showcase specific aspects of Scandinavian cuisine or cultural celebrations.

Reservations: Depending on the time and day you plan to dine, making reservations at Fika may be a good idea, especially during peak dining hours.

Friendly Staff: You can expect friendly and knowledgeable staff who are happy to explain the dishes and offer recommendations based on your preferences.

Take a Piece of Scandinavia Home: Some Scandinavian restaurants, including Fika, offer a selection of Nordic products for purchase, allowing you to take a piece of Scandinavia home with you.

Sampling Scandinavian cuisine at Fika is not just about enjoying a meal; it's a culinary journey that transports you to the flavors and traditions of the Nordic region. Whether you're a fan of Scandinavian food or a curious foodie looking to explore new tastes, Fika offers a warm and authentic dining experience in Minneapolis.

23.Dine at Spoon and Stable for a fine dining experience.

Dining at Spoon and Stable is a remarkable culinary journey that offers a refined and upscale fine dining experience in Minneapolis. Here's what you can expect when you dine at Spoon and Stable:

Sophisticated Atmosphere: Spoon and Stable is known for its elegant and sophisticated atmosphere. The restaurant is often praised for its stylish interior, which combines historic charm with modern design elements, creating a visually stunning dining environment.

Inventive Cuisine: The restaurant's menu features inventive and contemporary American cuisine with French influences. Chef Gavin Kaysen, a James Beard Award winner, curates a menu that highlights seasonal ingredients and showcases culinary creativity. Dishes are carefully crafted to provide a memorable and unique dining experience.

Tasting Menus: Spoon and Stable often offers tasting menus that allow you to explore a curated selection of dishes, each expertly paired with wines. Tasting menus provide an opportunity to savor a variety of flavors and culinary techniques.

Exceptional Wine List: The restaurant typically boasts an extensive wine list featuring a diverse range of wines from around the world. Knowledgeable sommeliers are available to assist with wine pairings that complement your meal.

Farm-to-Table Philosophy: Spoon and Stable places an emphasis on sourcing ingredients locally and sustainably. You can expect dishes made with fresh, seasonal, and locally produced ingredients.

Impeccable Service: The restaurant is known for its impeccable and attentive service. The staff is highly trained and aims to provide a memorable and personalized dining experience.

Private Dining: Spoon and Stable offers private dining options for special occasions, business gatherings, or intimate celebrations. Private dining rooms can accommodate both small and large groups.

Reservations Recommended: Due to its popularity and limited seating, making reservations at Spoon and Stable is highly recommended, especially for weekend dining.

Special Occasions: The restaurant is an ideal choice for celebrating special occasions, anniversaries, or romantic dinners. The ambiance and cuisine create a memorable backdrop for important moments.

Dress Code: Spoon and Stable typically has a dress code, so it's advisable to check in advance to ensure you're dressed appropriately for the fine dining setting.

Dessert and Pastry: Don't miss the opportunity to enjoy expertly crafted desserts and pastries, which are often a highlight of the dining experience.

Seasonal Variations: The menu at Spoon and Stable may change with the seasons, ensuring that you can savor the freshest and most in-season ingredients.

Dining at Spoon and Stable is a culinary adventure that combines exceptional cuisine, world-class service, and an inviting atmosphere. Whether you're a food enthusiast seeking a memorable dining experience or looking to celebrate a special occasion in style, Spoon and Stable delivers a sophisticated and unforgettable fine dining experience in Minneapolis.

24.Enjoy farm-to-table dining at The Bachelor Farmer.

Enjoying farm-to-table dining at The Bachelor Farmer is a culinary experience that celebrates the flavors of the Upper Midwest and showcases the concept of sustainability. Here's what you can expect when you dine at The Bachelor Farmer:

Farm-to-Table Philosophy: The Bachelor Farmer is renowned for its commitment to sourcing ingredients locally and sustainably. The restaurant works closely with regional farmers and producers to obtain fresh, seasonal, and high-quality ingredients. This philosophy is reflected in the menu, which features dishes made with the bounty of the Upper Midwest.

Seasonal Menus: The menu at The Bachelor Farmer changes with the seasons, allowing you to savor dishes that are inspired by the freshest ingredients available at any given time. This ensures that each visit can be a unique culinary experience.

Nordic Influence: The restaurant draws inspiration from Nordic cuisine and traditions, with a focus on simplicity and purity of flavors. You'll find dishes that showcase a combination of traditional Scandinavian elements and innovative culinary techniques.

Farm-Fresh Produce: The Bachelor Farmer often highlights farm-fresh produce in its dishes, including vegetables, fruits, and herbs sourced from local farms. This emphasis on fresh ingredients adds vibrancy and depth to the flavors.

Culinary Creativity: The chefs at The Bachelor Farmer are known for their culinary creativity and dedication to crafting dishes that are both visually stunning and delicious. The menu typically features a diverse range of options, including appetizers, main courses, and desserts.

Beverage Selection: The restaurant offers a thoughtfully curated beverage selection, including wines, craft beers, and cocktails that complement the menu.

Knowledgeable staff can assist with beverage pairings to enhance your dining experience.

Warm and Inviting Atmosphere: The Bachelor Farmer is housed in a historic building with a warm and inviting ambiance. The restaurant's design combines modern elements with rustic charm, creating an intimate and welcoming setting.

Community Focus: The restaurant is deeply connected to the local community and often participates in initiatives that support sustainability, local agriculture, and culinary education.

Reservations Recommended: Due to its popularity and limited seating, making reservations at The Bachelor Farmer is advisable, especially for dinner and weekend dining.

Special Occasions: The restaurant is an excellent choice for celebrating special occasions, anniversaries, or enjoying a romantic dinner. The combination of exceptional cuisine and a cozy atmosphere sets the stage for memorable dining experiences.

Desserts and Pastries: Don't miss the opportunity to explore the restaurant's dessert and pastry offerings, which are crafted with the same dedication to quality and creativity as the savory dishes.

Dining at The Bachelor Farmer allows you to experience the richness of the Upper Midwest's culinary heritage while embracing the farm-to-table movement and sustainable dining practices. Whether you're a food enthusiast seeking a taste of the region's best or simply looking for an exceptional dining experience, The Bachelor Farmer offers a memorable journey through the flavors of Minneapolis and the surrounding countryside.

25.Have brunch at Hell's Kitchen.

Having brunch at Hell's Kitchen is a popular and flavorful dining experience in Minneapolis that combines comfort food with a unique twist. Here's what you can expect when you enjoy brunch at Hell's Kitchen:

Comfort Food: Hell's Kitchen is known for its comfort food offerings, and the brunch menu is no exception. You can expect dishes like their famous lemon ricotta hotcakes, house-made corned beef hash, eggs Benedict, omelets, and more. Many items on the menu are made from scratch with a focus on quality and flavor.

Signature Bloody Mary Bar: Brunch at Hell's Kitchen often features a build-your-own Bloody Mary bar, allowing you to customize your cocktail with a variety of garnishes and mix-ins.

Vegetarian and Vegan Options: The menu typically includes vegetarian and vegan options, ensuring there's something for everyone, regardless of dietary preferences.

Warm and Rustic Atmosphere: Hell's Kitchen offers a warm and rustic ambiance with exposed brick walls and a cozy feel. It's a welcoming setting for a leisurely brunch with friends or family.

Live Music: On certain days, you might be treated to live music during brunch, adding to the lively and enjoyable atmosphere.

Variety of Breakfast Beverages: In addition to coffee and tea, Hell's Kitchen offers a range of breakfast beverages, including freshly squeezed orange juice and house-made ginger ale.

Artisanal Coffee: Coffee lovers can savor artisanal coffee brewed to perfection, often roasted on-site.

Specialty Pastries: The brunch menu sometimes features specialty pastries and baked goods. Be sure to inquire about any daily specials or unique offerings.

Local Ingredients: Hell's Kitchen is committed to sourcing local and sustainable ingredients whenever possible, which adds to the freshness and quality of their dishes.

Kid-Friendly: The restaurant is often considered kid-friendly, making it a good choice for family brunch outings.

Reservations: Given its popularity, making reservations for brunch at Hell's Kitchen is advisable, especially on weekends and during peak dining hours.

Award-Winning: Hell's Kitchen has received numerous awards and recognition for its food and dining experience, making it a must-visit for food enthusiasts.

Gift Shop: The restaurant often has a gift shop where you can purchase Hell's Kitchen-branded merchandise and culinary products.

Weekend Tradition: Brunch at Hell's Kitchen has become a beloved weekend tradition for many locals and visitors, offering a delicious and comforting start to the day.

Whether you're in the mood for classic brunch staples or unique and inventive dishes, Hell's Kitchen provides a memorable brunch experience that combines quality ingredients, flavor, and a welcoming atmosphere. It's a great place to enjoy a leisurely brunch while savoring the flavors of Minneapolis.

26.Savor a meal at Manny's Steakhouse.

Savoring a meal at Manny's Steakhouse is a culinary delight that offers an exceptional steakhouse experience in Minneapolis. Here's what you can expect when you dine at Manny's Steakhouse:

Prime Steaks: Manny's is renowned for its prime steaks, which are sourced from top-quality beef producers and aged to perfection. You can expect a selection of cuts, including ribeye, filet mignon, New York strip, and porterhouse, each prepared to your desired level of doneness.

Classic Steakhouse Atmosphere: The restaurant exudes a classic and upscale steakhouse atmosphere with dark wood paneling, plush leather seats, and a warm ambiance. It's an ideal setting for a special occasion, business dinner, or a romantic evening.

Seafood Selection: In addition to its steak offerings, Manny's typically features a variety of seafood options, including fresh seafood platters, lobster tail, and jumbo shrimp cocktail, allowing for a well-rounded dining experience.

Accompaniments: The menu includes a range of side dishes and accompaniments, such as creamed spinach, garlic mashed potatoes, and asparagus, to complement your steak.

Extensive Wine List: Manny's boasts an extensive wine list with a wide selection of red and white wines, as well as sommeliers who can assist with wine pairings to enhance your meal.

Signature Cocktails: The restaurant offers a selection of signature cocktails and a full bar, providing options for pre-dinner drinks or post-meal libations.

Dessert Indulgence: Be sure to leave room for dessert. Manny's typically offers a variety of indulgent desserts, including classic favorites like cheesecake and chocolate lava cake.

Impeccable Service: Manny's is known for its impeccable and attentive service. The staff is highly trained and dedicated to ensuring that every aspect of your dining experience is top-notch.

Private Dining: The restaurant often has private dining options for special events, parties, and gatherings. Private dining rooms can accommodate both small and large groups.

Reservations Recommended: Due to its popularity and limited seating, making reservations at Manny's Steakhouse is strongly recommended, especially for dinner and weekend dining.

Business-Friendly: Manny's is often frequented by business professionals and is known as a prime spot for business meetings and negotiations.

Awards and Accolades: The restaurant has received numerous awards and accolades for its steaks, wine selection, and overall dining experience.

Dining at Manny's Steakhouse is a treat for steak enthusiasts and anyone looking to indulge in a memorable steakhouse meal. It's a place where you can savor prime steaks, enjoy exceptional service, and immerse yourself in the classic steakhouse atmosphere, making it a standout dining destination in Minneapolis.

27.Taste local craft beer at Surly Brewing Company.

Tasting local craft beer at Surly Brewing Company is a must-do experience for beer enthusiasts visiting Minneapolis. Here's what you can expect when you visit Surly Brewing Company:

Craft Beer Selection: Surly Brewing Company is known for its diverse and innovative craft beer offerings. They typically have a rotating selection of beers on tap, including a wide range of styles such as IPAs, stouts, lagers, saisons, and more. Whether you're a fan of hoppy ales or prefer something maltier, you're likely to find a beer that suits your taste.

Brewery Atmosphere: The brewery often features a welcoming and vibrant atmosphere where you can relax, enjoy good company, and immerse yourself in the craft beer culture. The taproom is designed to provide a comfortable and enjoyable space for visitors.

Tours and Tastings: Surly Brewing Company typically offers brewery tours where you can learn about the beer-making process, the history of the brewery, and the company's commitment to quality. Tastings are often included in the tour experience, allowing you to sample a variety of their beers.

Outdoor Spaces: Depending on the season and weather, Surly Brewing Company may have outdoor spaces, such as patios or beer gardens, where you can sip your beer while enjoying the fresh air and socializing with fellow beer enthusiasts.

Food Options: The brewery often has on-site food options, ranging from casual pub fare to more upscale dining experiences. The food menu is designed to complement the beer offerings, allowing you to enjoy delicious pairings.

Events and Special Releases: Surly Brewing Company frequently hosts events, special beer releases, and themed gatherings. These events can be a great way to try unique and limited-edition brews while enjoying a lively atmosphere.

Merchandise and Swag: The brewery typically has a merchandise shop where you can purchase Surly Brewing Company-branded apparel, glassware, and other beer-related items as souvenirs.

Community and Local Engagement: Surly Brewing Company often supports and engages with the local community and charitable causes. Be sure to check if there are any events or initiatives taking place during your visit.

Family-Friendly: Some Surly Brewing Company locations are family-friendly, offering kid-friendly menus and activities to accommodate visitors of all ages.

Responsible Consumption: While enjoying craft beer, it's important to drink responsibly and be aware of your alcohol consumption. Many breweries, including Surly Brewing Company, promote responsible drinking practices.

Hours and Reservations: Check the brewery's hours of operation and whether reservations are required, especially during busy times or for brewery tours.

Sampling local craft beer at Surly Brewing Company is an opportunity to taste the creativity and craftsmanship of Minneapolis's thriving craft beer scene. Whether you're a seasoned beer connoisseur or just curious to explore new flavors, a visit to Surly Brewing Company can be a fun and flavorful experience.

28.Experience Middle Eastern cuisine at Holy Land.

Experiencing Middle Eastern cuisine at Holy Land is a flavorful journey that allows you to savor the rich and diverse flavors of the region. Here's what you can expect when you dine at Holy Land:

Authentic Middle Eastern Dishes: Holy Land offers a menu featuring a wide array of authentic Middle Eastern dishes that showcase the culinary traditions of the region. You can expect to find favorites like falafel, shawarma, kebabs, hummus, tabbouleh, baba ghanoush, and more.

Fresh Ingredients: The restaurant prides itself on using fresh and high-quality ingredients to create dishes that are both delicious and wholesome. The flavors are often enhanced by the use of aromatic spices and herbs.

Variety of Options: Holy Land typically provides a diverse menu with options for meat lovers, vegetarians, and vegans. Whether you prefer lamb, chicken, beef, or plant-based dishes, you'll have plenty of choices.

Bakery and Pastries: Holy Land often features a bakery section where you can indulge in fresh pita bread, pastries, and desserts. Baklava, a sweet pastry made with layers of filo dough, honey, and nuts, is a popular treat.

Mediterranean Influence: Middle Eastern cuisine often features Mediterranean influences, and you'll find dishes like Mediterranean salads and rice-based dishes on the menu.

Vibrant Spices: The cuisine is known for its vibrant and bold spices, which add depth and complexity to the flavors of the dishes. It's a cuisine that embraces a balance of savory, sour, and sweet elements.

Warm and Welcoming Atmosphere: Holy Land often provides a warm and welcoming atmosphere with Middle Eastern decor and music, creating an immersive dining experience.

Takeout and Grocery: Some Holy Land locations offer takeout and grocery options, allowing you to bring the flavors of the Middle East home with you. You can purchase spices, ingredients, and prepared dishes.

Cultural Experience: Dining at Holy Land offers a cultural experience that allows you to explore the food traditions and flavors of the Middle East without leaving Minneapolis.

Friendly Staff: The staff is often friendly and knowledgeable about the menu, making it easy to navigate the choices and receive recommendations.

Community Engagement: Holy Land is often involved in community initiatives and charitable efforts, contributing to the local community.

Catering: The restaurant may offer catering services, making it a great choice for events and gatherings where you want to treat guests to Middle Eastern cuisine.

Whether you're a longtime fan of Middle Eastern cuisine or new to the flavors of the region, dining at Holy Land provides an opportunity to savor dishes that are both delicious and culturally enriching. It's a place where you can enjoy the hospitality and culinary traditions of the Middle East in the heart of Minneapolis.

29. Visit the Midtown Global Market for international foods.

Visiting the Midtown Global Market is a culinary adventure that allows you to explore a world of international foods and flavors in the heart of Minneapolis. Here's what you can expect when you visit the Midtown Global Market:

Diverse Food Vendors: The Midtown Global Market is home to a diverse array of food vendors and artisans, representing cuisines and culinary traditions from around the world. You'll find stalls offering dishes from countries such as Mexico, India, Ethiopia, Thailand, Japan, and more.

Global Dining Experience: The market provides a unique dining experience where you can sample dishes from different regions and cultures, all in one location. It's an ideal destination for those who love to try new foods and flavors.

Variety of Cuisine: The market offers a wide variety of cuisine, including street food, comfort food, international classics, and fusion dishes. Whether you're in the mood for tacos, sushi, curry, or barbecue, you're likely to find it here.

Fresh and Authentic Ingredients: Many of the vendors at the Midtown Global Market use fresh and authentic ingredients to prepare their dishes, ensuring an authentic and flavorful experience.

Cafes and Bakeries: In addition to savory dishes, the market often features cafes and bakeries where you can enjoy coffee, pastries, desserts, and more.

Artisanal Products: Beyond food, the market may also host artisans selling handcrafted products, including jewelry, clothing, home goods, and unique gifts.

Casual Dining: The market typically has a casual and relaxed atmosphere, making it a great place for a quick bite, a leisurely meal, or even a family outing.

Community Events: The Midtown Global Market often hosts community events, cultural celebrations, and live performances, adding to the vibrancy and cultural richness of the space.

Outdoor Seating: Depending on the season, the market may offer outdoor seating areas, allowing you to dine al fresco and soak up the local atmosphere.

Family-Friendly: The market is often considered family-friendly, with options to satisfy even the pickiest eaters. It's a great place for families to explore and enjoy a variety of foods together.

International Grocery: Some vendors at the market may also sell international groceries, spices, and ingredients, allowing you to take a piece of global cuisine home with you.

Supporting Local Businesses: By dining at the Midtown Global Market, you're supporting local small businesses and entrepreneurs, contributing to the community's economic growth.

Whether you're on a culinary adventure or simply looking for a delicious and diverse dining experience, a visit to the Midtown Global Market offers a taste of the world's flavors without leaving Minneapolis. It's a hub of international cuisine, cultural exploration, and community engagement that food enthusiasts and visitors can appreciate.

30.Explore local food trucks for diverse culinary delights.

Exploring local food trucks in Minneapolis is a fantastic way to indulge in diverse culinary delights while immersing yourself in the city's vibrant street food scene. Here's what you can expect when you explore the local food trucks:

Diverse Cuisine: Minneapolis food trucks offer an incredibly diverse range of cuisine, from traditional favorites to creative and fusion dishes. You'll find everything from tacos, burgers, and barbecue to global fare like Thai, Korean, Middle Eastern, and more.

Unique Creations: Food trucks are known for their inventive and unique creations. Some trucks specialize in gourmet sandwiches, while others focus on gourmet donuts, gourmet grilled cheese, or other delicious specialties.

Fresh and Fast: Food trucks typically prepare dishes to order, ensuring that you receive freshly made food. It's a fast and convenient way to enjoy a meal on the go.

Local Ingredients: Many food truck operators source their ingredients locally, supporting regional farmers and producers. This commitment to using fresh, local ingredients often results in flavorful and high-quality dishes.

Food Truck Parks and Gatherings: Minneapolis often hosts food truck parks and gatherings, where multiple trucks come together in one location. These events create a festive and communal atmosphere, allowing you to sample a variety of foods in one visit.

Seasonal Specials: Some food trucks offer seasonal specials, taking advantage of the freshest ingredients available during different times of the year.

Vegetarian and Vegan Options: Food trucks typically cater to a variety of dietary preferences, so you can often find vegetarian and vegan options alongside traditional meat dishes.

Food Truck Festivals: Minneapolis hosts food truck festivals and events throughout the year, providing an opportunity to sample a wide range of dishes from different trucks in one place.

Supporting Local Businesses: By patronizing food trucks, you're supporting local small businesses and entrepreneurs who are passionate about their craft.

Creative Flavors: Food truck chefs often experiment with flavors, resulting in unique and memorable taste experiences. Be prepared to discover new flavor combinations and culinary surprises.

Social and Casual: Dining at food trucks is a social and casual experience. You can enjoy your meal at outdoor seating areas or simply take it with you to enjoy at a park or waterfront.

Local Recommendations: Don't hesitate to ask locals for their favorite food truck recommendations. They often have inside knowledge about hidden gems and must-try dishes.

Cash and Cards: While some food trucks are cash-only, many now accept credit and debit cards for convenience.

Exploring local food trucks in Minneapolis is an adventure for your taste buds, offering a wide range of flavors and culinary creations. Whether you're strolling through the city or attending a food truck event, you'll have the opportunity to savor diverse and delicious dishes while enjoying the lively street food culture of Minneapolis.

31.Catch a live comedy show at Acme Comedy Co.

Catching a live comedy show at Acme Comedy Co. is a guaranteed way to have a night filled with laughter and entertainment in Minneapolis. Here's what you can expect when you attend a comedy show at Acme Comedy Co.:

Travel to Minneapolis Minnesota

Top-Notch Comedians: Acme Comedy Co. is known for hosting both nationally recognized and up-and-coming comedians. You can expect to see talented performers who have appeared on television, in movies, and on comedy specials. The lineup often includes a diverse range of comedic styles and perspectives.

Intimate Venue: Acme Comedy Co. typically offers an intimate and cozy setting, allowing for a more personal and engaging comedy experience. The close proximity to the stage makes you feel like part of the show.

Diverse Comedy Styles: Comedy shows at Acme often feature a mix of comedic styles, including stand-up, improvisation, and sketch comedy. You'll have the opportunity to enjoy a variety of comedic performances in one place.

Live Audience Interaction: Comedians at Acme frequently engage with the audience, creating memorable and interactive moments that add to the fun. Be prepared for good-natured banter and spontaneous laughter.

Full-Service Bar: The venue usually has a full-service bar, allowing you to enjoy drinks while you watch the show. It's a great way to relax and enhance your comedy experience.

Special Events and Headliners: Acme Comedy Co. occasionally hosts special events, themed shows, and headlining comedians. These events can offer a unique and elevated comedy experience.

Reservations Recommended: Due to the popularity of the comedy club, it's often advisable to make reservations, especially if you plan to attend on a weekend or during a special event.

Age Restrictions: Comedy shows at Acme Comedy Co. are typically intended for mature audiences. Check the age restrictions before attending with younger guests.

Laughter Therapy: Enjoying a live comedy show can be a form of laughter therapy, offering stress relief, relaxation, and a memorable night out.

Local Comedy Scene: Minneapolis has a thriving comedy scene, and Acme Comedy Co. is a significant part of it. Supporting local comedians and comedy venues contributes to the vibrancy of the community.

Gift of Laughter: Comedy show tickets can make great gifts for friends, family, or anyone in need of a good laugh.

Check the Schedule: Be sure to check the schedule in advance to see which comedians will be performing during your visit. You might discover a favorite comedian or an act you've been eager to see.

Arrive Early: Arriving a bit early allows you to secure good seating and enjoy pre-show drinks and conversation with fellow comedy enthusiasts.

Catching a live comedy show at Acme Comedy Co. is a fantastic way to unwind, share laughs with friends, and experience the humor of talented comedians. Whether you're a seasoned comedy aficionado or simply in need of a good laugh, Acme Comedy Co. provides an enjoyable and memorable night of entertainment in Minneapolis.

32.Dance the night away at The Exchange & Alibi Lounge.

Dancing the night away at The Exchange & Alibi Lounge is a fantastic way to experience the vibrant nightlife of Minneapolis. Here's what you can expect when you visit The Exchange & Alibi Lounge:

Dual Venues: The Exchange & Alibi Lounge often consist of two interconnected venues, providing a diverse nightlife experience. The Exchange is a high-energy dance club, while Alibi Lounge offers a more relaxed and lounge-style atmosphere. You can choose the ambiance that suits your mood.

Live DJs: The venues typically feature live DJs who spin a wide range of music genres, including electronic dance music (EDM), hip-hop, pop, house, and more. The music sets the tone for a night of dancing and entertainment.

Dance Floor: The Exchange is known for its spacious dance floor, where you can dance to the latest beats and mingle with fellow partygoers. The energetic atmosphere and lighting effects create an immersive dance experience.

VIP Sections: If you prefer a more exclusive experience, The Exchange & Alibi Lounge often have VIP sections with bottle service available. It's a great option for special occasions or groups looking for a private space.

Signature Cocktails: Alibi Lounge typically offers a menu of signature cocktails and craft beverages, allowing you to enjoy expertly crafted drinks while socializing.

Themed Events: The venues occasionally host themed events, parties, and special performances. Check their event calendar to see if there's a particular theme or guest artist you'd like to catch.

Late-Night Hours: The Exchange & Alibi Lounge often stay open late into the night, making them ideal destinations for those looking to dance and enjoy the nightlife until the early hours.

Diverse Crowd: You'll find a diverse and lively crowd at The Exchange & Alibi Lounge, creating a dynamic and inclusive atmosphere.

Dress Code: Be sure to check the dress code, as some nights may have specific attire requirements. Dressing stylishly is often encouraged.

Cover Charge: There may be a cover charge to enter the venues, especially on busy nights or during special events. Consider checking their website or contacting them in advance for details.

Safety and Security: The venues typically prioritize the safety and security of their patrons, with trained staff and security measures in place.

Special Occasions: The Exchange & Alibi Lounge are often chosen for celebrating special occasions, birthdays, bachelorette parties, and other milestones.

Public Transit: Consider using public transportation or rideshare services if you plan to enjoy the nightlife and need a safe way to get home after a night of dancing.

Dancing the night away at The Exchange & Alibi Lounge is an exciting and immersive experience for those looking to have a memorable night out in Minneapolis. Whether you're a dance enthusiast or simply want to enjoy the music and energy of the crowd, these venues offer a dynamic and entertaining nightlife destination.

33.Attend a live music show at Icehouse.

Attending a live music show at Icehouse is a memorable and immersive experience that allows you to enjoy the vibrant music scene in Minneapolis. Here's what you can expect when you attend a live music show at Icehouse:

Live Music Venue: Icehouse is a renowned live music venue in Minneapolis known for hosting a wide range of musical genres and performances. The venue typically features local, national, and international artists, showcasing diverse musical talents.

Intimate Setting: Icehouse provides an intimate and cozy setting for live music performances. The smaller venue size allows for a closer connection between the artists and the audience, creating an immersive and engaging experience.

Eclectic Lineup: The venue often features an eclectic lineup of musicians, including jazz, indie, rock, electronic, folk, and experimental acts. You can explore different musical genres and discover new artists while enjoying a night out.

Full-Service Restaurant and Bar: Icehouse is not only a music venue but also a full-service restaurant and bar. You can enjoy dinner and drinks before or during the show, making it a convenient and enjoyable night out.

Late-Night Shows: Some live music performances at Icehouse are held later in the evening, making it a great destination for those looking to enjoy music and entertainment into the night.

Local Talent: Icehouse frequently showcases local talent from the thriving Minneapolis music scene. It's an excellent opportunity to support emerging artists and enjoy homegrown talent.

Upcoming Artists: The venue often hosts up-and-coming artists and bands, offering a chance to catch live performances by musicians who may be on the cusp of wider recognition.

Ticketing: Tickets for live music shows at Icehouse are typically available for purchase in advance. Be sure to check the venue's website or contact them directly for ticketing information and show schedules.

Food and Drink Menu: Icehouse typically offers a menu of creative dishes and craft cocktails. It's a great place to enjoy a meal or try specialty drinks while listening to live music.

Cozy Atmosphere: The atmosphere at Icehouse is often described as cozy and welcoming, creating a comfortable and enjoyable space for music enthusiasts.

Seating Options: Depending on the event and the layout, Icehouse may offer a combination of seated and standing room areas. Check the seating arrangements for the specific show you plan to attend.

Local Art: The venue occasionally features local artwork, adding to the artistic and creative ambiance of the space.

Check the Schedule: Be sure to check Icehouse's schedule and event calendar to see which artists and bands will be performing during your visit. You might find a show that aligns with your musical preferences.

Attending a live music show at Icehouse is a fantastic way to immerse yourself in the local music scene, discover new talent, and enjoy an intimate and engaging musical experience in Minneapolis. Whether you're a music aficionado or simply looking for a memorable night out, Icehouse provides a platform for musical exploration and enjoyment.

34.Enjoy karaoke at The Shout! House.

Enjoying karaoke at The Shout! House is a lively and interactive experience that adds a dose of musical fun to your night out in Minneapolis. Here's what you can expect when you visit The Shout! House for karaoke:

Dueling Pianos: The Shout! House is known for its dueling pianos concept, where talented pianists take center stage and perform a wide range of songs based on audience requests. The pianists often engage in friendly musical competition, creating an entertaining and dynamic atmosphere.

Live Music and Sing-Along: While The Shout! House primarily features dueling pianos, it's also a place where you can join in and sing along with the performers. Karaoke-style moments may be interspersed throughout the night, allowing you and fellow patrons to take the mic and showcase your vocal talents.

Song Requests: You can request your favorite songs, and the pianists typically do their best to accommodate a variety of musical preferences. It's an interactive experience where audience participation is encouraged.

Diverse Song Selection: The song selection at The Shout! House often spans various genres and decades, so you can expect to hear classic hits, contemporary tunes, rock anthems, pop favorites, and more.

Audience Engagement: The pianists and staff often engage with the audience, creating a lively and fun atmosphere. You might find yourself participating in sing-alongs, dance-offs, and musical challenges.

Celebrations and Special Occasions: The Shout! House is a popular destination for celebrating special occasions, birthdays, bachelorette parties, and other milestones. You can reserve tables or sections for your group to ensure a memorable celebration.

Late-Night Entertainment: The venue often hosts late-night entertainment, making it a great spot for those who want to enjoy music and karaoke well into the night.

Full Bar and Drink Specials: The Shout! House typically has a full bar, offering a variety of cocktails, beer, and other beverages. Drink specials and promotions may be available during certain hours or events.

Audience Participation: If you're feeling brave, you can volunteer to sing your favorite songs during karaoke moments. It's all in good fun, and the audience is generally supportive and enthusiastic.

Reservations and Cover Charge: Depending on the night and the event, The Shout! House may have a cover charge or require reservations. It's a good idea to check their website or contact them in advance for details.

Party Atmosphere: The Shout! House often exudes a party atmosphere, with a high-energy crowd looking to have a good time. It's a place where you can let loose and enjoy the music.

Experiencing karaoke at The Shout! House is an opportunity to sing your heart out, dance the night away, and revel in the joy of live music and audience interaction. Whether you're a seasoned karaoke enthusiast or a first-time performer, it's a fun and entertaining way to spend an evening in Minneapolis.

35.Play arcade games at Up-Down Minneapolis.

Playing arcade games at Up-Down Minneapolis is a nostalgic and entertaining experience that combines classic games with a lively and social atmosphere. Here's what you can expect when you visit Up-Down Minneapolis:

Classic Arcade Games: Up-Down Minneapolis is known for its extensive collection of classic arcade games from the '80s and '90s. You can enjoy a wide variety of games, including classics like Pac-Man, Donkey Kong, Space Invaders, Galaga, pinball machines, and many more. The arcade games are well-maintained and ready for you to play.

Token System: Typically, Up-Down operates on a token system. You exchange cash for tokens, which you can then use to play the games. It's a simple and convenient way to enjoy the arcade.

Selection of Craft Beers: The venue often features a great selection of craft beers on tap, allowing you to enjoy a cold brew while you play. The beer offerings can include local and regional options.

Retro Aesthetic: Up-Down Minneapolis often has a retro and nostalgic aesthetic, with vintage arcade cabinets, neon lights, and '80s and '90s memorabilia. It creates a fun and immersive environment for gamers of all ages.

Social Setting: Up-Down is often a social destination where you can hang out with friends, challenge fellow gamers to friendly competitions, and meet like-minded individuals who share your passion for arcade gaming.

Live Music and Events: The venue occasionally hosts live music events, DJ nights, and special events. Be sure to check their event calendar for any upcoming shows or themed parties.

Late-Night Fun: Up-Down Minneapolis typically stays open late into the night, making it an ideal spot for late-night entertainment and a unique alternative to traditional nightlife options.

Snacks and Pizza: Some Up-Down locations offer a menu of snacks, pizza, and other comfort food options to keep you fueled for your gaming sessions.

Private Events and Parties: Up-Down often accommodates private events and parties, making it a popular choice for birthday celebrations, corporate events, and gatherings with friends.

Competitions and Tournaments: Depending on the night, you might find arcade game competitions or tournaments taking place. It's a chance to test your skills and win prizes.

Family-Friendly Hours: While Up-Down is often a popular spot for adults, it may offer family-friendly hours where younger gamers can join in the fun.

Cover Charge: Some special events or late-night hours may have a cover charge, so it's a good idea to check their website or contact them for details before planning your visit.

Playing arcade games at Up-Down Minneapolis is a blast from the past that provides hours of entertainment and a nostalgic trip down memory lane. Whether you're a seasoned gamer or simply looking for a fun and social activity, Up-Down offers a unique and enjoyable experience in Minneapolis.

36.Try your luck at Mystic Lake Casino.

Trying your luck at Mystic Lake Casino is a thrilling and entertaining experience for those looking to enjoy gaming and entertainment in the Minneapolis area. Here's what you can expect when you visit Mystic Lake Casino:

Gaming Variety: Mystic Lake Casino typically offers a wide variety of gaming options, including slot machines, table games like blackjack, poker, roulette, and more. Whether you're a novice or experienced gambler, you'll find games that suit your preferences and skill level.

Slot Machines: The casino typically features a large selection of slot machines, ranging from traditional reel slots to modern video slots with exciting themes and bonus features.

Table Games: If you enjoy table games, you can usually find a range of options, from classic card games like blackjack and poker to games of chance like roulette and craps.

Poker Room: Mystic Lake often has a dedicated poker room where you can participate in poker tournaments or enjoy cash games with fellow players.

Bingo: Some Mystic Lake Casino locations also have bingo halls, offering a fun and social way to try your luck.

Entertainment and Shows: In addition to gaming, the casino often hosts live entertainment, concerts, comedy shows, and special events. Check their event calendar to see if there are any performances or shows happening during your visit.

Dining Options: The casino typically offers a variety of dining options, from casual eateries to upscale restaurants. You can enjoy a meal or snack while taking a break from gaming.

Bars and Lounges: Mystic Lake often has bars and lounges where you can relax with a drink and socialize with other patrons.

Hotel Accommodations: If you're planning an extended stay, Mystic Lake Casino often has on-site hotel accommodations, providing convenience for guests who want to make the most of their visit.

Promotions and Rewards: Many casinos, including Mystic Lake, have player reward programs and promotions that offer perks and incentives for frequent visitors.

Responsible Gaming: While gaming can be a lot of fun, it's important to gamble responsibly. Mystic Lake Casino typically provides resources and information about responsible gaming practices.

Age Restrictions: Casinos usually have age restrictions, with entry limited to individuals who are 18 or 21 years of age or older. Make sure to check the age requirements before planning your visit.

Security and Safety: Casinos often prioritize the safety and security of their patrons, with trained staff and security measures in place.

Special Events: Mystic Lake Casino may host special events, such as casino tournaments or themed nights, which can add to the excitement of your visit.

Before planning your trip to Mystic Lake Casino, it's a good idea to check their website or contact them for information on gaming options, promotions, dining, entertainment, and any COVID-19 protocols that may be in place. Whether you're a seasoned gambler or simply looking for a night of entertainment, Mystic Lake Casino offers a wide range of experiences for visitors seeking their luck in Minneapolis.

37.Attend a sports game at Target Field or U.S. Bank Stadium.

Attending a sports game at Target Field or U.S. Bank Stadium is a thrilling experience for sports enthusiasts in Minneapolis. Here's what you can expect when you attend a game at these iconic venues:

Target Field (Home of the Minnesota Twins - MLB):

Baseball Atmosphere: Target Field provides an authentic and lively baseball atmosphere, with a picturesque view of the Minneapolis skyline as a backdrop.
Seating Options: The stadium offers a range of seating options, from traditional stadium seats to premium club seating with access to exclusive amenities.
Food and Beverages: You'll find a diverse selection of food and beverage options, including classic ballpark fare, local favorites, and craft beer selections.
Entertainment: Between innings, enjoy entertainment, fan contests, and the traditional seventh-inning stretch.
Family-Friendly: Target Field is family-friendly, with designated areas for kids, such as the family fun zone.
Merchandise: Team merchandise and souvenirs are available for purchase, allowing you to support the Twins in style.
U.S. Bank Stadium (Home of the Minnesota Vikings - NFL):

Football Excitement: U.S. Bank Stadium is known for its electric football atmosphere, making it an ideal destination for NFL games.
Seating Experience: The stadium offers a variety of seating options, from standard seats to luxury suites, providing diverse perspectives of the action.
Concessions: Enjoy a wide array of food and beverage options, including classic stadium snacks, local specialties, and craft beer selections.
Halftime Shows: NFL games often feature exciting halftime shows, performances, and entertainment.

Tailgating: Many fans gather in the parking lots surrounding the stadium for pre-game tailgating festivities.

Merchandise: Team merchandise shops offer a range of Vikings gear and apparel for fans to show their support.

Game Day Experience:

Tailgating: Depending on the sport and the venue, tailgating may be a popular pre-game tradition, offering a chance to socialize and enjoy food and drinks before the game.

Fan Engagement: Fans at both stadiums are known for their passionate support of their teams, creating a spirited and lively atmosphere.

Game-Day Rituals: Witnessing fan traditions and rituals, such as the "Skol Chant" for the Vikings, adds to the excitement of attending a game.

Tickets and Timing:

It's advisable to purchase tickets well in advance, especially for popular games or matchups.

Check the game schedule, as well as any pre-game events or promotions that may be taking place.

COVID-19 Considerations:

Be aware of any COVID-19 protocols or restrictions in place at the time of your visit, as they may affect seating capacity, mask requirements, and other safety measures.

Attending a sports game at Target Field or U.S. Bank Stadium allows you to immerse yourself in the excitement of professional sports in Minneapolis. Whether you're a die-hard fan or simply looking for a memorable sporting event, these stadiums offer an unforgettable game-day experience in the heart of the city.

38.Experience the nightlife in the North Loop district.

Experiencing the nightlife in the North Loop district of Minneapolis is a vibrant and dynamic way to enjoy the city's entertainment scene. Here's what you can expect when you venture into the North Loop for a night out:

Hip and Trendy Atmosphere: The North Loop is known for its hip and trendy atmosphere, making it a popular destination for locals and visitors looking for a stylish night on the town.

Diverse Dining Options: The district boasts an array of restaurants and eateries offering diverse cuisine options. Whether you're in the mood for upscale dining, contemporary American fare, international flavors, or creative small plates, you'll find it in the North Loop.

Craft Cocktails and Bars: The North Loop is home to craft cocktail bars and speakeasies where mixologists create signature drinks and cocktails. It's a great place to enjoy a unique beverage in a sophisticated setting.

Live Music and Entertainment: Depending on the night, you might find live music performances, DJ sets, or other entertainment at various bars and venues in the North Loop. Check out the local event listings for upcoming shows and performances.

Art Galleries and Studios: The district often features art galleries and studios, contributing to its creative and artistic vibe. You can explore contemporary art exhibitions or even attend gallery openings.

Rooftop Bars: Some North Loop establishments have rooftop bars or outdoor seating areas, allowing you to enjoy your drinks with a view of the city skyline.

Late-Night Hours: Many bars and restaurants in the North Loop stay open late into the night, making it a prime destination for those who want to experience Minneapolis nightlife.

Fashion Boutiques: If you're into fashion and shopping, you'll find boutique shops and clothing stores in the area, offering unique and stylish finds.

Walking and Exploring: The North Loop is a walkable district, making it easy to hop from one venue to another. Stroll along the cobblestone streets and explore the neighborhood's charm.

Local Breweries: Minneapolis is known for its craft beer scene, and you can find local breweries and taprooms in the North Loop where you can sample a variety of beer styles.

Local Events and Festivals: The North Loop often hosts local events and festivals, including art fairs, food festivals, and cultural celebrations. Check the event calendar to see if there's an event happening during your visit.

Transportation: Consider using rideshare services, public transportation, or designated drivers if you plan to enjoy the nightlife and want a safe way to get home.

Dress to Impress: Depending on the venue, you may want to dress up a bit for a night out in the North Loop. Some places have a chic dress code.

Reservations: For popular restaurants and bars, it's advisable to make reservations in advance, especially on weekends.

Experiencing the nightlife in the North Loop district is a memorable way to enjoy Minneapolis after dark. Whether you're looking for a fine dining experience, craft cocktails, live music, or simply a trendy atmosphere to unwind, the North Loop offers a wide range of options to suit your nightlife preferences.

39.Check out a burlesque show at Lush Bar.

Checking out a burlesque show at Lush Bar is a delightful and entertaining experience in Minneapolis. Here's what you can expect when you attend a burlesque show at Lush Bar:

Burlesque Entertainment: Lush Bar is known for hosting captivating and visually stunning burlesque performances. Burlesque is an art form that combines elements of comedy, dance, and striptease, often with elaborate costumes and theatrical flair.

Talented Performers: The burlesque shows at Lush Bar typically feature talented and charismatic performers who bring unique acts to the stage. You can expect a diverse range of acts, from classic burlesque to modern and innovative performances.

Variety of Acts: Burlesque shows often include a variety of acts, each with its own theme, style, and music. These acts can range from humorous and cheeky to sensual and glamorous.

Live Music and Dance: Some burlesque shows incorporate live music and dance, enhancing the overall experience and adding to the atmosphere.

Audience Interaction: Burlesque shows often involve audience interaction, with performers engaging the crowd in a playful and entertaining manner. Be prepared for good-natured banter and audience participation.

Full-Service Bar: Lush Bar typically has a full-service bar where you can enjoy a wide selection of beverages, including cocktails, beer, wine, and non-alcoholic options.

Intimate Setting: Lush Bar provides an intimate and cozy setting for burlesque shows, allowing for a closer connection between the performers and the audience. It creates an immersive and engaging experience.

Themed Shows: Depending on the night, Lush Bar may host themed burlesque shows, which can add an extra layer of excitement and creativity to the performance.

Reservations: It's advisable to make reservations, especially if you plan to attend on a popular night or for a specific show. Reservations ensure you have a seat and can enjoy the performance comfortably.

Age Restrictions: Burlesque shows are typically intended for mature audiences, so be sure to check the age restrictions before attending with younger guests.

Support for Local Artists: Lush Bar often supports local burlesque artists and performers, contributing to the local arts and entertainment scene.

Special Occasions: Burlesque shows can make for a unique and memorable celebration for special occasions, birthdays, bachelorette parties, and more. Consider booking a table for a group celebration.

Check the Schedule: Be sure to check Lush Bar's schedule and event calendar to see which burlesque shows and performers will be featured during your visit. You might discover a show that aligns with your preferences.

Attending a burlesque show at Lush Bar is an opportunity to enjoy the art of tease, comedy, and dance while celebrating the creativity and talent of local performers. Whether you're a seasoned burlesque enthusiast or simply looking for a night of entertainment, Lush Bar provides an intimate and captivating burlesque experience in Minneapolis.

40.Explore the craft cocktail scene at Marvel Bar.

Exploring the craft cocktail scene at Marvel Bar is a sophisticated and delightful experience for cocktail enthusiasts in Minneapolis. Here's what you can expect when you visit Marvel Bar:

Craft Cocktails: Marvel Bar is renowned for its craft cocktails, meticulously created by skilled mixologists who take pride in their craft. The menu often features a curated selection of inventive and expertly crafted drinks.

Creative Ingredients: You'll find cocktails at Marvel Bar that incorporate unique and high-quality ingredients, including house-made syrups, bitters, infusions, and artisanal spirits. The creativity of the cocktails is part of what sets the bar apart.

Signature Cocktails: Marvel Bar typically has a list of signature cocktails that showcase the bar's distinct style and innovation. These cocktails may change seasonally, offering a reason to return and try new creations.

Bespoke Cocktails: If you have specific preferences or flavors in mind, Marvel Bar's mixologists are often open to crafting bespoke cocktails tailored to your taste.

Expert Mixologists: The bartenders at Marvel Bar are skilled and knowledgeable about the art of mixology. They can offer recommendations, share insights about the cocktails, and create personalized drinks based on your preferences.

Intimate Setting: Marvel Bar often provides an intimate and upscale setting for patrons to enjoy their drinks. The ambiance is conducive to savoring and appreciating the craftsmanship that goes into each cocktail.

Attention to Detail: The attention to detail in the presentation of cocktails at Marvel Bar is remarkable. You can expect garnishes, glassware, and drink presentation that elevate the overall experience.

Seasonal Ingredients: The bar may incorporate seasonal and locally sourced ingredients into its cocktails, ensuring a fresh and evolving menu.

Pairing with Food: Some craft cocktails are designed to complement the flavors of the food menu if Marvel Bar offers dining options. Pairing cocktails with food can enhance the overall dining experience.

Bar Snacks: To accompany your cocktails, Marvel Bar may offer a selection of bar snacks or small plates. These snacks can be a delightful accompaniment to your drinks.

Reservations Recommended: Due to its popularity and limited seating capacity, it's often advisable to make reservations, especially if you plan to visit during peak hours or on weekends.

Cocktail Classes and Events: Depending on the season, Marvel Bar may host cocktail classes, workshops, or special events that allow patrons to learn more about mixology and cocktail preparation.

Artistic Presentation: The presentation of cocktails at Marvel Bar is often artistic and visually appealing, making the experience all the more enjoyable.

Attention to Service: The staff at Marvel Bar typically provides attentive and personalized service, ensuring that your visit is memorable and enjoyable.

Dress Code: Marvel Bar may have a dress code that encourages a more upscale and stylish appearance, so consider dressing accordingly.

Exploring the craft cocktail scene at Marvel Bar is a journey into the world of artisanal cocktails and mixology. Whether you're a cocktail connoisseur or simply looking for a refined and upscale drinking experience, Marvel Bar offers a unique and memorable opportunity to savor exceptional cocktails in Minneapolis.

41.Tour the Minneapolis Central Library.

Touring the Minneapolis Central Library is a fascinating way to explore the city's literary and architectural treasures. Here's what you can expect when you visit the Minneapolis Central Library:

Architectural Marvel: The Minneapolis Central Library is known for its striking and modern architectural design. The building features a unique combination of glass, metal, and concrete, making it an architectural marvel in downtown Minneapolis. Be sure to take in the building's exterior design, as it's a sight to behold.

Interior Atrium: Upon entering the library, you'll find an impressive atrium with a soaring glass ceiling. The atrium is often flooded with natural light, creating a welcoming and airy atmosphere.

Book Collections: The library houses an extensive collection of books, magazines, periodicals, and other reading materials. Whether you're interested in fiction, non-fiction, reference materials, or research resources, you'll find a wealth of literary options.

Special Collections: Minneapolis Central Library often features special collections and archives that cater to various interests, including local history, genealogy, rare books, and more. Be sure to inquire about any special exhibitions or displays during your visit.

Technology and Multimedia: In addition to traditional books, the library provides access to computers, e-books, audiobooks, and multimedia resources. You can use library computers for research, work, or internet browsing.

Meeting Spaces: The library may offer meeting rooms, study areas, and collaborative spaces for public use. These spaces are often equipped with technology and can be reserved for meetings or group work.

Children's and Teen Sections: Families can explore dedicated sections for children and teenagers, featuring age-appropriate books, educational resources, and interactive activities.

Events and Programs: Minneapolis Central Library frequently hosts events, workshops, author talks, and educational programs for all ages. Check the library's event calendar to see if there are any interesting programs happening during your visit.

Art Installations: The library often features art installations and exhibits that add to the cultural ambiance of the space. These installations may showcase the work of local artists or explore various themes.

Café and Refreshments: Some libraries have on-site cafes or areas where you can grab a coffee or a snack to enjoy during your visit.

Library Services: The library provides a range of services, including reference assistance, library card registration, interlibrary loan, and more. Librarians are typically available to help with research or information needs.

Accessibility: The library is typically designed to be accessible to all visitors, including those with disabilities. Check with library staff for any specific accessibility accommodations you may require.

Guided Tours: The library may offer guided tours led by knowledgeable staff or volunteers. These tours can provide insight into the library's history, architecture, and resources.

Quiet and Reading Areas: For those seeking a tranquil environment for reading or study, the library often designates quiet zones and reading areas where you can immerse yourself in your chosen reading materials.

Hours of Operation: Be sure to check the library's website or contact them directly for their hours of operation, as they may vary depending on the day and any special events.

Touring the Minneapolis Central Library is not only an opportunity to explore a wealth of literary resources but also a chance to appreciate modern architecture and engage in educational and cultural activities. Whether you're a bibliophile, a history enthusiast, or simply looking for a peaceful place to read, the library offers a welcoming and enriching experience in downtown Minneapolis.

42. Learn about the city's milling history at the Mill City Museum.

Learning about the city's milling history at the Mill City Museum is a captivating journey into Minneapolis's rich industrial heritage. Here's what you can expect when you visit the Mill City Museum:

Historic Mill Building: The Mill City Museum is housed in the ruins of what was once the Washburn "A" Mill, a historic flour mill complex. The museum itself is an architectural marvel, preserving the industrial character of the original building.

Flour Milling History: The museum offers a comprehensive exploration of Minneapolis's role as the flour milling capital of the world during the late 19th and early 20th centuries. You'll learn about the rise of the milling industry and how it shaped the city's development.

Travel to Minneapolis Minnesota

Interactive Exhibits: The Mill City Museum features a range of interactive exhibits that bring the history of flour milling to life. These exhibits often include multimedia presentations, artifacts, and hands-on activities that engage visitors of all ages.

Flour Tower Elevator Tour: One of the highlights of the museum is the Flour Tower Elevator Tour. Visitors are guided through the history of flour milling as they ride an elevator up the inside of the mill. The tour offers panoramic views of the Mississippi River and the milling district.

Historic Machinery: You can expect to see historic milling machinery, equipment, and artifacts on display, giving you a glimpse into the milling process that was once an integral part of Minneapolis's economy.

Riverfront Location: The Mill City Museum is situated along the scenic Mississippi River waterfront, providing picturesque views and the opportunity to explore the riverfront area.

Educational Programs: The museum often offers educational programs and workshops for visitors of all ages, making it a great destination for families and school groups.

Special Exhibitions: Depending on the season and schedule, the museum may host special exhibitions related to milling history, local culture, and other relevant topics.

Mill Ruins Park: Adjacent to the museum, you'll find Mill Ruins Park, which features the preserved ruins of the historic Washburn "A" Mill and other milling-related structures. It's an excellent place to take a leisurely stroll and appreciate the industrial history of the area.

Gift Shop: The museum typically has a gift shop where you can purchase books, souvenirs, and locally sourced products related to milling history and Minneapolis.

Visitor Center: The visitor center provides information about the museum, its exhibits, and the surrounding area. You can obtain tickets and plan your visit here.

Hours and Admission: Be sure to check the museum's website for hours of operation, admission fees, and any special events or exhibitions that may be taking place during your visit.

Accessibility: The museum is designed to be accessible to all visitors, including those with disabilities. Check with museum staff for any specific accessibility accommodations you may require.

Visiting the Mill City Museum is an opportunity to step back in time and gain a deeper understanding of how Minneapolis played a pivotal role in the development of the milling industry. It's a fascinating and educational experience that offers a glimpse into the city's industrial past.

43.Visit the Minnesota History Center in St. Paul.

Visiting the Minnesota History Center in St. Paul is a captivating way to explore the rich history and cultural heritage of the state of Minnesota. Here's what you can expect when you visit the Minnesota History Center:

Historical Exhibits: The Minnesota History Center typically features a wide range of historical exhibits that delve into various aspects of Minnesota's past. These exhibits often cover topics such as Native American history, pioneer life, industry, transportation, politics, and social movements.

Interactive Displays: Many of the exhibits at the History Center are interactive, providing visitors with hands-on experiences, multimedia presentations, and opportunities to engage with historical artifacts and documents.

Rotating Exhibitions: The museum often hosts rotating exhibitions that showcase diverse aspects of Minnesota history, including art, culture, sports, and contemporary issues. These exhibitions change periodically, offering returning visitors something new to explore.

Archives and Collections: The Minnesota History Center houses an extensive collection of historical documents, photographs, manuscripts, and artifacts. Researchers and history enthusiasts can access these materials for in-depth exploration.

Permanent Displays: The museum typically has permanent displays that highlight key moments in Minnesota's history, from its early settlement to its role in national events.

Travel to Minneapolis Minnesota

Cultural Heritage: You can learn about the diverse cultural heritage of Minnesota, including the contributions of various immigrant groups and communities that have shaped the state's identity.

Family-Friendly: The Minnesota History Center often provides family-friendly exhibits and activities, making it an ideal destination for visitors of all ages. There are often interactive spaces designed for children to learn about history through play.

Educational Programs: The History Center offers a variety of educational programs, workshops, and lectures for school groups, families, and individuals interested in deepening their understanding of Minnesota's history.

Museum Store: The museum typically has a museum store where you can purchase books, gifts, and merchandise related to Minnesota history and culture.

Café: Some visitors' centers have a café or dining area where you can enjoy a meal or refreshments during your visit.

Events and Special Programs: The Minnesota History Center often hosts events, lectures, and special programs related to historical topics and contemporary issues. Check their event calendar for any upcoming programs or activities.

Visitor Center: The visitor center provides information about the museum, its exhibits, hours of operation, and admission fees. You can obtain tickets and plan your visit here.

Accessibility: The museum is designed to be accessible to all visitors, including those with disabilities. Check with museum staff for any specific accessibility accommodations you may require.

Hours and Admission: Be sure to check the Minnesota History Center's website for hours of operation, admission fees, and any special exhibitions or events that may be taking place during your visit.

Exploring the Minnesota History Center in St. Paul is a journey through time, offering a deeper appreciation of the state's history, culture, and contributions to the nation. Whether you're a history enthusiast, a student, or simply looking for an enriching cultural experience, the History Center provides a valuable opportunity to connect with Minnesota's past.

44.Explore the Somali Museum of Minnesota.

Exploring the Somali Museum of Minnesota is an opportunity to learn about the rich culture, history, and contributions of the Somali community in the state. Here's what you can expect when you visit the Somali Museum of Minnesota:

Cultural Exhibits: The museum typically features cultural exhibits that showcase various aspects of Somali culture, including art, music, dance, clothing, language, and traditions. These exhibits provide insights into the vibrant heritage of the Somali people.

Historical Displays: You can learn about the history of Somalia and the journey of Somali immigrants and refugees to Minnesota. Historical displays may cover topics such as the Somali Civil War, migration stories, and the experiences of Somalis in their new homeland.

Artifacts and Artwork: The museum often displays a collection of artifacts, traditional Somali artwork, textiles, and crafts. These items offer a glimpse into the artistic and creative expressions of the Somali culture.

Interactive Learning: Some exhibits may include interactive elements that allow visitors to engage with the culture and history of Somalia. Interactive displays can make the learning experience more immersive and engaging.

Storytelling and Oral History: The Somali Museum of Minnesota often places a strong emphasis on oral history and storytelling. You may have the opportunity to listen to personal narratives and stories from members of the Somali community, providing a deeper understanding of their experiences and perspectives.

Educational Programs: The museum typically offers educational programs, workshops, and events that promote cross-cultural understanding and celebrate the diversity of Minnesota. These programs may include lectures, cultural performances, and hands-on activities.

Community Engagement: The museum often serves as a hub for community engagement, providing a space for cultural events, gatherings, and discussions. It's a place where the Somali community in Minnesota can come together and share their heritage.

Gift Shop: Some visitors' centers have a gift shop where you can purchase books, crafts, and merchandise related to Somali culture and history.

Diversity and Inclusion: The Somali Museum of Minnesota aims to promote diversity and inclusion by fostering dialogue and understanding between the Somali community and the broader Minnesota community.

Visitor Center: The visitor center provides information about the museum, its exhibits, hours of operation, and admission fees. You can obtain tickets and plan your visit here.

Hours and Admission: Be sure to check the Somali Museum of Minnesota's website or contact them directly for hours of operation, admission fees, and any special exhibitions or events that may be taking place during your visit.

Exploring the Somali Museum of Minnesota is a unique and enlightening experience that allows you to gain a deeper appreciation of the Somali culture, history, and the vibrant community that calls Minnesota home. It's a place where cultural exchange and understanding flourish, making it a valuable destination for those interested in exploring diverse perspectives and traditions.

45.Discover the Bakken Museum of Electricity.

Discovering the Bakken Museum of Electricity is a fascinating exploration of the history of electricity, science, and innovation. Here's what you can expect when you visit the Bakken Museum:

History of Electricity: The Bakken Museum typically features exhibits that delve into the history of electricity, exploring its discovery, development, and impact on society. You'll learn about the pioneers and inventors who shaped the field of electrical science.

Hands-On Science: The museum often provides interactive and hands-on science exhibits that allow visitors of all ages to engage with electrical phenomena and conduct experiments. These exhibits make learning about electricity fun and engaging.

Medical Electricity: The Bakken Museum has a special focus on medical electricity and its historical applications in medicine. You can learn about early electrotherapy devices, medical innovations, and the evolution of medical technology.

Artifacts and Inventions: The museum houses a collection of artifacts, electrical devices, and inventions related to electricity and science. These items offer insights into the technological advancements that have occurred over the years.

Nikola Tesla Collection: Some Bakken Museum locations may have a dedicated Nikola Tesla collection, featuring artifacts and information about the life and work of the renowned inventor.

Outdoor Space: Depending on the location, the Bakken Museum may have outdoor spaces, gardens, or scenic areas where you can relax and enjoy the surroundings.

Educational Programs: The museum often offers educational programs, workshops, and demonstrations that cater to students, families, and science enthusiasts. These programs can deepen your understanding of electrical science and its applications.

Special Exhibitions: Check the museum's schedule for any special exhibitions or events that may be taking place during your visit. These exhibitions can provide additional insights into the world of electricity and innovation.

Gift Shop: Some visitors' centers have a gift shop where you can purchase science-related books, gadgets, and educational materials.

Visitor Center: The visitor center provides information about the museum, its exhibits, hours of operation, and admission fees. You can obtain tickets and plan your visit here.

Accessibility: The museum is typically designed to be accessible to all visitors, including those with disabilities. Check with museum staff for any specific accessibility accommodations you may require.

Hours and Admission: Be sure to check the Bakken Museum's website for hours of operation, admission fees, and any special programs or events that may be happening during your visit.

Exploring the Bakken Museum of Electricity is a journey into the world of science and innovation, offering a deeper understanding of electricity's role in shaping our modern world. Whether you're a science enthusiast, a student, or simply curious about the history of electrical science, the Bakken Museum provides an enlightening and engaging experience.

46.Learn about Minnesota's Jewish history at the Jewish Historical Society of the Upper Midwest.

Learning about Minnesota's Jewish history at the Jewish Historical Society of the Upper Midwest is a meaningful exploration of the contributions, heritage, and experiences of the Jewish community in the region. Here's what you can expect when you visit the Jewish Historical Society:

Historical Exhibits: The Jewish Historical Society typically features exhibits that delve into the history of Jewish communities in the Upper Midwest. These exhibits often cover topics such as immigration, settlement, religious life, cultural traditions, and notable individuals.

Photographs and Artifacts: The museum houses a collection of photographs, artifacts, documents, and memorabilia that provide a visual and tangible connection to the past. These items help tell the story of the Jewish community's journey and experiences in the region.

Oral Histories: Some exhibits may incorporate oral histories and personal narratives from members of the Jewish community, offering a firsthand perspective on their experiences, traditions, and contributions.

Cultural Celebrations: The museum often showcases cultural celebrations, festivals, and traditions of the Jewish community, allowing visitors to learn about holidays, rituals, and customs.

Educational Programs: The Jewish Historical Society typically offers educational programs, lectures, workshops, and events that promote an understanding of Jewish history and culture. These programs cater to various age groups and interests.

Community Engagement: The museum serves as a hub for community engagement, providing a space for cultural events, discussions, and gatherings that celebrate the Jewish heritage.

Research Resources: Researchers and history enthusiasts may have access to research materials, archives, and libraries related to Jewish history and genealogy.

Gift Shop: Some visitors' centers have a gift shop where you can purchase books, Judaica, and items related to Jewish culture and history.

Visitor Center: The visitor center provides information about the museum, its exhibits, hours of operation, and admission fees. You can obtain tickets and plan your visit here.

Accessibility: The museum is typically designed to be accessible to all visitors, including those with disabilities. Check with museum staff for any specific accessibility accommodations you may require.

Hours and Admission: Be sure to check the Jewish Historical Society's website or contact them directly for hours of operation, admission fees, and any special exhibitions or events that may be taking place during your visit.

Exploring the Jewish Historical Society of the Upper Midwest is a meaningful way to gain insight into the Jewish community's history, culture, and contributions in the region. It offers an opportunity for cultural exchange, education, and appreciation of the rich and diverse tapestry of Minnesota's history.

47. Visit the Hennepin History Museum.

Visiting the Hennepin History Museum is a wonderful way to explore the history and heritage of Hennepin County, including Minneapolis and its surrounding areas. Here's what you can expect when you visit the Hennepin History Museum:

Local History Exhibits: The museum typically features a range of exhibits that showcase the history of Hennepin County. These exhibits may cover topics such as the early settlement, industrialization, immigration, social movements, and significant events that have shaped the region.

Historical Artifacts: You can expect to see a collection of historical artifacts, photographs, documents, and memorabilia that provide insights into the county's past. These items help bring history to life and create a tangible connection to the region's heritage.

Interactive Displays: Some exhibits at the museum may incorporate interactive elements, multimedia presentations, and hands-on activities that engage visitors and make the learning experience more immersive.

Rotating Exhibitions: The Hennepin History Museum often hosts rotating exhibitions that explore specific aspects of local history in greater detail. These exhibitions change periodically, offering returning visitors something new to discover.

Community Stories: The museum may feature community stories and personal narratives from individuals who have lived in Hennepin County, providing a diverse and multifaceted perspective on the region's history.

Educational Programs: The museum typically offers educational programs, lectures, workshops, and events that cater to a variety of age groups and interests. These programs can deepen your understanding of Hennepin County's history and culture.

Genealogy and Research: Researchers and history enthusiasts may have access to research materials, archives, and resources related to Hennepin County's history and genealogy.

Gift Shop: Some visitors' centers have a gift shop where you can purchase books, souvenirs, and merchandise related to local history and culture.

Visitor Center: The visitor center provides information about the museum, its exhibits, hours of operation, and admission fees. You can obtain tickets and plan your visit here.

Accessibility: The museum is typically designed to be accessible to all visitors, including those with disabilities. Check with museum staff for any specific accessibility accommodations you may require.

Hours and Admission: Be sure to check the Hennepin History Museum's website or contact them directly for hours of operation, admission fees, and any special exhibitions or events that may be taking place during your visit.

Visiting the Hennepin History Museum is an opportunity to delve into the rich history of Hennepin County and gain a deeper appreciation of the people, events, and stories that have shaped the region. Whether you're a local resident or a visitor interested in regional history, the museum provides an enriching and educational experience.

48.Explore the Firefighters Hall and Museum.

Exploring the Firefighters Hall and Museum is a captivating journey into the history and heroism of firefighting in Minneapolis and beyond. Here's what you can expect when you visit the Firefighters Hall and Museum:

Historical Exhibits: The museum typically features a range of exhibits that delve into the history of firefighting, with a particular focus on Minneapolis and the surrounding areas. These exhibits may cover the evolution of firefighting equipment, the development of fire departments, and the challenges firefighters have faced over the years.

Antique Fire Apparatus: One of the highlights of the museum is its collection of antique fire apparatus, including vintage fire engines, hoses, helmets, and other firefighting equipment. These well-preserved artifacts offer a glimpse into the technology and tools used by firefighters in the past.

Interactive Displays: Some exhibits at the museum may incorporate interactive elements, allowing visitors to engage with firefighting equipment, simulate fire rescue scenarios, and learn about fire safety practices.

Firefighter Memorabilia: The Firefighters Hall and Museum often houses a collection of firefighter memorabilia, including patches, uniforms, badges, and personal items that belonged to firefighters. These items help tell the stories of the brave men and women who have served in the profession.

Educational Programs: The museum typically offers educational programs, workshops, and events that provide insights into firefighting history and safety. These programs can be both entertaining and informative for visitors of all ages.

Fire Safety Education: As part of its mission, the museum often emphasizes fire safety education. You may find displays and resources that promote fire prevention and safety practices for families and individuals.

Special Exhibitions: Check the museum's schedule for any special exhibitions or events that may be taking place during your visit. These exhibitions can provide additional insights into the world of firefighting.

Gift Shop: Some visitors' centers have a gift shop where you can purchase firefighting-themed books, apparel, and souvenirs.

Visitor Center: The visitor center provides information about the museum, its exhibits, hours of operation, and admission fees. You can obtain tickets and plan your visit here.

Accessibility: The museum is typically designed to be accessible to all visitors, including those with disabilities. Check with museum staff for any specific accessibility accommodations you may require.

Hours and Admission: Be sure to check the Firefighters Hall and Museum's website or contact them directly for hours of operation, admission fees, and any special programs or events that may be happening during your visit.

Exploring the Firefighters Hall and Museum is an opportunity to honor the bravery and dedication of firefighters while gaining a deeper understanding of the history and challenges of firefighting. Whether you have a personal connection to the profession or simply appreciate the heroism of firefighters, the museum offers an informative and inspiring experience.

49. Discover the history of music at the Schubert Club Museum.

Discovering the history of music at the Schubert Club Museum is a delightful journey through the world of classical music and musical instruments. Here's what you can expect when you visit the Schubert Club Museum:

Historical Musical Instruments: The museum typically features a collection of historical musical instruments, including pianos, harpsichords, violins, and other instruments that have played a role in the history of music. These instruments often span different time periods and styles, allowing you to see how music and instrument design have evolved over the years.

Rare Manuscripts and Scores: You can expect to find rare manuscripts, original musical scores, and sheet music that showcase the work of renowned composers. These documents provide insights into the composition process and the music of different eras.

Composer Memorabilia: The museum may house memorabilia related to famous composers, such as letters, personal items, and artifacts associated with composers like Franz Schubert, whose name the museum carries.

Interactive Exhibits: Some exhibits at the Schubert Club Museum may incorporate interactive elements, allowing visitors to explore the sounds of different musical instruments and learn about musical concepts.

Historical Context: The museum often places music in its historical context, providing information about the social, cultural, and artistic influences that shaped musical compositions and performances.

Educational Programs: The museum typically offers educational programs, workshops, and events that cater to music enthusiasts, students, and families. These programs can deepen your understanding of classical music and its history.

Musical Performances: Depending on the museum's schedule, you may have the opportunity to attend musical performances, recitals, or lectures that showcase the talents of local musicians and highlight specific aspects of classical music.

Special Exhibitions: Check the museum's schedule for any special exhibitions or events related to music history, classical composers, or musical genres. These exhibitions can provide additional insights into the world of music.

Gift Shop: Some visitors' centers have a gift shop where you can purchase music-related books, recordings, and souvenirs.

Visitor Center: The visitor center provides information about the museum, its exhibits, hours of operation, and admission fees. You can obtain tickets and plan your visit here.

Accessibility: The museum is typically designed to be accessible to all visitors, including those with disabilities. Check with museum staff for any specific accessibility accommodations you may require.

Hours and Admission: Be sure to check the Schubert Club Museum's website or contact them directly for hours of operation, admission fees, and any special concerts or events that may be taking place during your visit.

Exploring the Schubert Club Museum is a chance to immerse yourself in the beauty and history of classical music. Whether you're a classical music aficionado or simply curious about the world of music, the museum offers a rich and inspiring experience.

50.Tour the Wells Fargo History Museum.

Touring the Wells Fargo History Museum provides a unique opportunity to delve into the history of banking, the Wells Fargo company, and the role it played in the development of the American West. Here's what you can expect when you visit the Wells Fargo History Museum:

Historical Exhibits: The museum typically features a range of exhibits that trace the history of Wells Fargo, from its founding during the Gold Rush era to its evolution as a modern banking and financial services company. These exhibits often cover topics such as stagecoach transportation, early banking operations, and the growth of the Wells Fargo network.

Stagecoach Display: One of the highlights of the museum is the display of a vintage Wells Fargo stagecoach, which provides a tangible connection to the company's iconic role in stagecoach transportation during the 19th century.

Interactive Displays: Some exhibits at the Wells Fargo History Museum may incorporate interactive elements, allowing visitors to explore the workings of a stagecoach, learn about banking services, and experience the challenges of the Gold Rush era.

Historical Documents and Artifacts: You can expect to see historical documents, photographs, banking ledgers, and artifacts related to the Wells Fargo company and its operations throughout its history.

Gold Rush Era: The museum often places a strong emphasis on the Gold Rush era and the crucial role Wells Fargo played in transporting gold, providing financial services, and supporting the growth of Western communities during that time.

Educational Programs: The museum typically offers educational programs, workshops, and events that provide insights into the history of banking, the Gold Rush, and the Wells Fargo company. These programs may cater to students, families, and history enthusiasts.

Community Engagement: The Wells Fargo History Museum serves as a resource for community engagement, often hosting events, lectures, and discussions that explore various aspects of American history and finance.

Gift Shop: Some visitors' centers have a gift shop where you can purchase books, souvenirs, and merchandise related to Wells Fargo's history and the American West.

Visitor Center: The visitor center provides information about the museum, its exhibits, hours of operation, and admission fees. You can obtain tickets and plan your visit here.

Accessibility: The museum is typically designed to be accessible to all visitors, including those with disabilities. Check with museum staff for any specific accessibility accommodations you may require.

Hours and Admission: Be sure to check the Wells Fargo History Museum's website or contact them directly for hours of operation, admission fees, and any special programs or events that may be happening during your visit.

Touring the Wells Fargo History Museum is an opportunity to step back in time and learn about the fascinating history of banking, transportation, and the American West. Whether you're interested in financial history, the Gold Rush, or the development of the American frontier, the museum offers an informative and engaging experience.

51.Shop for local goods at the Minneapolis Farmers Market.

Shopping for local goods at the Minneapolis Farmers Market is a delightful and authentic way to experience the vibrant culture and agricultural bounty of the region. Here's what you can expect when you visit the Minneapolis Farmers Market:

Travel to Minneapolis Minnesota

Fresh Produce: The market is renowned for its wide selection of fresh fruits and vegetables. Depending on the season, you can find everything from crisp apples and sweet corn to ripe tomatoes and colorful peppers. Locally grown produce is a highlight of the market.

Local Artisans: In addition to produce, the market often features local artisans and crafters who offer a variety of handmade products. This may include artisanal cheeses, homemade jams and preserves, baked goods, handcrafted jewelry, and more.

Farm-Fresh Meats: Many vendors at the market sell farm-fresh meats, including beef, pork, poultry, and lamb. You can find a range of cuts and specialty products from local farms.

Flowers and Plants: The Minneapolis Farmers Market is a great place to shop for fresh flowers and plants. You can discover seasonal blooms and greenery to brighten up your home or garden.

Food Trucks and Prepared Foods: Some markets have food trucks and vendors offering delicious ready-to-eat meals, snacks, and beverages. It's an excellent opportunity to savor local flavors and cuisine.

Artisanal Products: You may find vendors selling artisanal products such as honey, maple syrup, herbal teas, and handmade soaps. These items often make for unique and thoughtful gifts.

Seasonal Offerings: The market's offerings change with the seasons. In the summer, you can enjoy a wide variety of fresh, ripe produce, while in the fall, you'll find an abundance of pumpkins and gourds.

Local Community: Visiting the Minneapolis Farmers Market is a chance to connect with local farmers, producers, and community members. You can chat with the people who grow and create the goods you're purchasing.

Events and Festivals: Throughout the year, the market may host special events, festivals, and themed markets that celebrate holidays, local traditions, or specific products.

Family-Friendly Atmosphere: The market is often family-friendly, and children can enjoy activities like face painting, live music, and entertainment.

Scenic Setting: Depending on the location you visit, the market may be set in a picturesque outdoor space, providing a pleasant environment for shopping and strolling.

Ample Parking: Some market locations offer ample parking for visitors' convenience.

Sustainability: Many vendors at the market prioritize sustainable and organic farming practices, making it a great place to support eco-conscious agriculture.

Visitor Information: Look for information booths or visitor centers at the market, where you can obtain maps, learn about market rules, and get tips on what's in season.

Hours and Location: Be sure to check the Minneapolis Farmers Market's website or contact them directly for information on market hours, locations, and any specific guidelines or events.

Visiting the Minneapolis Farmers Market is an enjoyable and enriching experience that allows you to savor the flavors of the region, support local producers, and immerse yourself in the community spirit of Minneapolis. Whether you're shopping for fresh ingredients or simply exploring the market's offerings, it's a must-visit destination for locals and visitors alike.

52.Explore the Mall of America for shopping and entertainment.

Exploring the Mall of America is a comprehensive shopping and entertainment experience in Bloomington, Minnesota. Here's what you can expect when you visit the Mall of America:

Shopping: The Mall of America is one of the largest shopping malls in the United States, boasting over 5.6 million square feet of retail space. You'll find a diverse array of stores, ranging from popular national brands and luxury boutiques to specialty shops and unique local retailers. Whether you're looking for fashion, electronics, home decor, or something entirely unique, the mall offers a vast selection of goods.

Entertainment: The mall is a hub of entertainment options for visitors of all ages. Some of the key entertainment attractions include:

Nickelodeon Universe: An indoor amusement park featuring thrilling rides, attractions, and character meet-and-greets. It's a hit with families and kids.

SEA LIFE Minnesota: An underwater adventure featuring a stunning aquarium with a variety of marine life, including sharks, rays, and sea turtles. Visitors can walk through a tunnel surrounded by aquatic creatures.

FlyOver America: A virtual flight experience that takes you on an exhilarating journey across the United States, immersing you in breathtaking landscapes.

Mini Golf: Enjoy a round of mini golf at Moose Mountain Adventure Golf, an 18-hole course with scenic waterfalls and challenging holes.

Crayola Experience: A creative and colorful attraction where you can participate in hands-on activities, create your own art, and explore the world of Crayola.

The Escape Game: Challenge yourself with immersive escape room experiences, solving puzzles and riddles to complete your mission.

Theatres: Catch the latest blockbuster movies at the mall's movie theaters, which offer comfortable seating and state-of-the-art technology.

Dining: The Mall of America is home to a wide range of dining options, from quick bites and fast food to sit-down restaurants and fine dining establishments. You can find cuisine from around the world, catering to various tastes and dietary preferences.

Events and Special Occasions: The mall often hosts events, promotions, and special occasions throughout the year. These can include fashion shows, live performances, holiday celebrations, and more. Check the mall's website or event calendar for the latest updates.

Visitor Services: The mall provides visitor services, including information desks, stroller rentals, wheelchair services, and foreign currency exchange.

Accessibility: The Mall of America is designed to be accessible to all visitors, including those with disabilities. It offers accessible restrooms, elevators, and parking spaces.

Parking: The mall has ample parking facilities with multiple entrances and ramps for easy access.

Hours: Mall hours may vary, so it's advisable to check the Mall of America's official website or contact them directly for current hours of operation and any special guidelines.

Exploring the Mall of America is a comprehensive and enjoyable experience that offers a wide range of shopping, dining, and entertainment options under one roof. Whether you're looking for a day of retail therapy, family fun, or a memorable dining experience, the mall has something to offer for everyone.

53. Visit the Midtown Global Market for unique items.

Visiting the Midtown Global Market is an exciting opportunity to explore a diverse and vibrant marketplace in Minneapolis, Minnesota. Here's what you can expect when you visit the Midtown Global Market:

Cultural Diversity: The Midtown Global Market celebrates cultural diversity by bringing together a wide range of food vendors, artisans, and businesses representing various ethnic backgrounds. It's a melting pot of global flavors, traditions, and products.

Food Vendors: The market is known for its diverse and delicious food offerings. You can sample cuisine from different parts of the world, including Mexican, Somali, Thai, Middle Eastern, and many others. Whether you're in the mood for savory dishes, sweet treats, or international delicacies, you'll find a variety of options.

Artisans and Boutiques: The Midtown Global Market features artisanal shops and boutiques where you can browse and purchase unique items such as clothing, jewelry, home decor, and gifts. These shops often showcase handmade and locally crafted products.

Global Flavors: The market is a culinary adventure, with vendors offering a wide range of global flavors and dishes. You can enjoy authentic Mexican tacos, Somali sambusas, Thai curries, Middle Eastern kebabs, and more. It's a great place for food enthusiasts to explore new tastes.

Live Entertainment: Depending on the day and time of your visit, you may be treated to live entertainment, including music, dance performances, and cultural events that add to the vibrant atmosphere of the market.

Community Events: The Midtown Global Market frequently hosts community events, workshops, and cultural celebrations that provide insights into various traditions and promote cross-cultural understanding.

Art Exhibits: Some parts of the market may feature art exhibits and displays that showcase the work of local artists and photographers. It's a dynamic space where creativity and culture converge.

Community Gathering Place: The market serves as a community gathering place, bringing together people from diverse backgrounds to share their culinary traditions, stories, and experiences.

Accessibility: The Midtown Global Market is designed to be accessible to all visitors, including those with disabilities.

Visitor Information: Look for information booths or visitor centers where you can obtain maps, learn about special events, and get recommendations for vendors to visit.

Hours and Location: Be sure to check the Midtown Global Market's website or contact them directly for hours of operation, directions, and any specific guidelines or events that may be happening during your visit.

Visiting the Midtown Global Market is an enriching experience that allows you to celebrate cultural diversity, savor global flavors, and discover unique items from around the world. Whether you're looking for a culinary adventure, one-of-a-kind gifts, or a lively and inclusive atmosphere, the market has something to offer for everyone.

54. Stroll through the North Loop's boutique shops.

Strolling through the North Loop's boutique shops in Minneapolis is a delightful way to discover unique fashion, home decor, and artisanal products. Here's what you can expect when you explore the North Loop's boutique shops:

Fashion Boutiques: The North Loop is known for its stylish fashion boutiques, featuring clothing, footwear, and accessories for men and women. You can find a curated selection of trendy and timeless pieces from local designers and independent brands.

Home Decor and Furnishings: Many boutiques in the North Loop offer a range of home decor and furnishings that cater to various tastes and design aesthetics. You can discover vintage and modern pieces, unique artwork, and interior decor items to enhance your living space.

Artisanal Goods: The neighborhood is home to boutiques that specialize in artisanal products, such as handcrafted jewelry, ceramics, candles, and other locally made items. These boutiques often showcase the craftsmanship and creativity of local artisans.

Antique Shops: Antique enthusiasts can explore shops in the North Loop that offer a selection of antique furniture, collectibles, and vintage items. It's a treasure trove for those looking to add a touch of history to their homes.

Local and Independent Designers: The North Loop supports local and independent designers, and you can find boutiques that exclusively feature their creations. This is an excellent place to discover unique and one-of-a-kind pieces.

Pop-Up Shops and Art Galleries: The neighborhood's creative spirit extends to pop-up shops and art galleries that frequently showcase emerging artists and designers. These spaces provide an ever-changing selection of art, fashion, and design.

Cafes and Eateries: As you explore the North Loop's boutique shops, you'll also encounter charming cafes and eateries where you can take a break, enjoy a cup of coffee, or savor a delicious meal.

Cultural Events: Depending on the time of year, the North Loop may host cultural events, art exhibitions, and neighborhood festivals that celebrate local creativity and community engagement.

Community Atmosphere: The North Loop is known for its friendly and community-oriented atmosphere. Shopkeepers are often passionate about their products and eager to share stories and recommendations with visitors.

Accessibility: The North Loop's boutiques are typically located in a walkable area, and most shops are designed to be accessible to all visitors.

Hours: Boutique hours may vary, so it's advisable to check with individual shops or the North Loop's official website for current hours of operation and any special events.

Strolling through the North Loop's boutique shops is a rewarding experience that allows you to support local businesses, discover unique treasures, and immerse yourself in the neighborhood's artistic and creative vibe. Whether you're shopping for fashion, home decor, or simply exploring the area, the North Loop offers a charming and distinctive retail experience.

55.Shop for vintage finds at Rewind Minneapolis.

Shopping for vintage finds at Rewind Minneapolis is a nostalgic and treasure-hunting experience in the city. Here's what you can expect when you visit Rewind Minneapolis:

Vintage Clothing: Rewind Minneapolis is known for its curated collection of vintage clothing and accessories. You can browse through racks of clothing items that span different eras, from the 1920s to the 1990s and beyond. Vintage dresses, suits, hats, and accessories are among the highlights.

Unique Vintage Styles: Whether you're looking for the elegance of the 1950s, the boldness of the 1970s, or the grunge of the 1990s, Rewind typically offers a diverse selection of styles that capture the fashion trends of each era.

Vintage Accessories: In addition to clothing, you can find a variety of vintage accessories such as handbags, shoes, scarves, and jewelry that complement your retro look or add a unique touch to your modern wardrobe.

Vintage Home Decor: Some vintage shops, including Rewind, may also feature a selection of vintage home decor items. You can discover mid-century furniture, retro kitchenware, vintage posters, and other items to enhance your living space.

Vinyl Records: Rewind Minneapolis may also offer a selection of vinyl records, allowing music enthusiasts to explore classic albums and discover hidden gems from various musical genres.

Collectibles and Memorabilia: Vintage shops often carry collectible items, memorabilia, and vintage toys that appeal to collectors and nostalgia seekers.

One-of-a-Kind Finds: Shopping at Rewind is like embarking on a treasure hunt. Each visit may reveal one-of-a-kind pieces and unexpected gems that you won't find in mainstream stores.

Knowledgeable Staff: Vintage shopkeepers are often passionate about the items they curate and can provide insights into the history and significance of the pieces they offer. Feel free to ask questions and learn more about the vintage finds.

Sustainability: Vintage shopping is a sustainable and eco-friendly choice, as it promotes the reuse and repurposing of pre-loved items, reducing the environmental impact of fast fashion.

Accessibility: Rewind Minneapolis is typically designed to be accessible to all visitors, including those with disabilities.

Hours: Vintage shop hours may vary, so it's a good idea to check Rewind Minneapolis's website or contact them directly for current hours of operation.

Shopping for vintage finds at Rewind Minneapolis is a journey through the past, offering a chance to embrace timeless styles, rediscover the aesthetics of previous decades, and find unique pieces that reflect your personal style. Whether you're a seasoned vintage enthusiast or new to the world of retro fashion, Rewind offers a curated selection of items that celebrate the beauty and history of vintage fashion and design.

56.Explore the locally owned stores on Nicollet Avenue.

Exploring the locally owned stores on Nicollet Avenue in Minneapolis is a wonderful way to discover unique products, support local businesses, and immerse yourself in the community. Here's what you can expect when you explore Nicollet Avenue's locally owned stores:

Diverse Shopping: Nicollet Avenue is known for its diverse range of locally owned shops and boutiques. As you stroll down the avenue, you can expect to find a wide variety of stores offering everything from clothing and accessories to home decor, gifts, and specialty items.

Unique Products: The locally owned stores on Nicollet Avenue often carry unique and one-of-a-kind products that you won't find in large chain retailers. These products may be crafted by local artisans, designers, and makers, making them extra special.

Boutiques and Fashion: Nicollet Avenue is home to several boutique clothing stores that showcase the latest fashion trends, vintage finds, and handcrafted apparel. You can explore local fashion designers and discover clothing that suits your style.

Art Galleries: Some stores on Nicollet Avenue may double as art galleries, showcasing the work of local artists. You can admire and purchase original artwork, sculptures, and other creative pieces.

Home Decor and Furnishings: If you're looking to enhance your living space, you'll find locally owned stores offering a range of home decor items, furniture, and accessories that cater to various design preferences.

Gift Shops: Nicollet Avenue's shops often have a selection of unique and locally made gifts, perfect for special occasions or souvenirs. You may find items like handmade candles, pottery, jewelry, and more.

Food and Specialty Stores: Some stores may focus on gourmet food products, specialty spices, teas, and other culinary delights. These shops are a great place to discover unique ingredients for your cooking and baking needs.

Bookstores: Nicollet Avenue may have locally owned bookstores where you can browse a curated selection of books, including novels, non-fiction, and titles by local authors.

Friendly Atmosphere: Nicollet Avenue's locally owned stores often have a welcoming and community-oriented atmosphere. Shopkeepers are typically passionate about their products and may offer personalized service and recommendations.

Accessibility: Most stores on Nicollet Avenue are designed to be accessible to all visitors, including those with disabilities.

Hours: Store hours can vary, so it's advisable to check with individual shops or the Nicollet Avenue business association for current hours of operation.

Community Events: Depending on the season and local events, Nicollet Avenue may host street fairs, sidewalk sales, and community gatherings. These events can be a great opportunity to explore the avenue's offerings and engage with the local community.

Exploring the locally owned stores on Nicollet Avenue is a rewarding experience that allows you to connect with the creativity and entrepreneurship of local businesses. Whether you're shopping for fashion, home decor, gifts, or simply enjoying a leisurely stroll, Nicollet Avenue offers a charming and diverse retail experience in Minneapolis.

57.Check out the Minneapolis Craft Market.

Checking out the Minneapolis Craft Market is a delightful way to explore local craftsmanship, discover unique handmade products, and support local artisans. Here's what you can expect when you visit the Minneapolis Craft Market:

Local Artisans: The Minneapolis Craft Market typically features a diverse group of local artisans, makers, and crafters who showcase their handmade products. You can meet the talented individuals behind the creations and learn about their craft.

Handcrafted Goods: The market offers a wide variety of handcrafted goods, including jewelry, ceramics, textiles, candles, soaps, woodworking, leather goods, and more. These products often reflect the creativity and craftsmanship of the artisans.

Unique and One-of-a-Kind Items: If you're looking for unique and one-of-a-kind items, the craft market is an ideal place to shop. You can find distinctive pieces that make for meaningful gifts or additions to your own collection.

Travel to Minneapolis Minnesota

Artistic Expression: The market celebrates artistic expression and provides a platform for local artists and artisans to share their work with the community. It's an opportunity to explore different styles, techniques, and artistic visions.

Artisan Demonstrations: Depending on the market's schedule, you may have the chance to witness live artisan demonstrations, allowing you to see the creative process in action and gain insights into traditional and contemporary craft techniques.

Food and Beverages: Some craft markets include food vendors and beverage options, making it a convenient and enjoyable outing where you can grab a snack or refreshment while shopping.

Community Atmosphere: Craft markets often have a friendly and community-oriented atmosphere. It's a place where you can connect with fellow art enthusiasts, learn about the local arts scene, and engage with the makers themselves.

Seasonal and Themed Markets: Depending on the time of year, the Minneapolis Craft Market may host seasonal or themed markets that focus on specific holidays, occasions, or artistic themes. These events can provide a unique shopping experience.

Family-Friendly: Craft markets are often family-friendly, with activities and offerings that appeal to visitors of all ages. Some markets may have activities for kids, making it a fun outing for families.

Accessibility: Craft markets are typically designed to be accessible to all visitors, including those with disabilities.

Hours: Craft market hours may vary, so it's a good idea to check the Minneapolis Craft Market's website or contact them directly for current hours of operation and any upcoming events.

Visiting the Minneapolis Craft Market is a celebration of local creativity, craftsmanship, and artistry. Whether you're seeking unique gifts, home decor, or simply appreciate the skill and passion of artisans, the craft market offers a vibrant and enriching shopping experience in Minneapolis.

58.Visit the Minneapolis Convention Center's gift shops.

Visiting the Minneapolis Convention Center's gift shops is a convenient way to find souvenirs, local products, and memorabilia related to the city. Here's what you can expect when you explore the gift shops at the Minneapolis Convention Center:

Local Merchandise: The gift shops typically offer a selection of locally sourced merchandise that represents the culture, landmarks, and spirit of Minneapolis. You can find items like Minneapolis-themed clothing, mugs, magnets, postcards, and more.

Convention Center Souvenirs: As a visitor to the Minneapolis Convention Center, you can pick up convention-specific souvenirs and memorabilia to commemorate your visit or attend an event.

Minnesota and Twin Cities Memorabilia: The gift shops may also carry items that celebrate the state of Minnesota and the Twin Cities area, allowing you to take home a piece of the region's identity.

Books and Literature: Some gift shops may offer books, publications, and literature that highlight the history, culture, and attractions of Minneapolis and its surroundings.

Art and Local Crafts: Depending on the shop's offerings, you might find locally crafted artwork, jewelry, and handicrafts that showcase the talents of Minnesota artists and artisans.

Apparel and Accessories: If you're looking for Minneapolis-themed clothing, accessories, or apparel with a local flair, the gift shops may have options that suit your style.

Snacks and Treats: Some gift shops offer locally made snacks and treats, providing a taste of Minnesota's culinary delights.

Visitor Information: The gift shops may serve as a source of visitor information, offering maps, brochures, and guides to help you make the most of your time in Minneapolis.

Accessibility: The Minneapolis Convention Center's gift shops are typically designed to be accessible to all visitors, including those with disabilities.

Hours: Gift shop hours may vary, so it's a good idea to check with the Minneapolis Convention Center or visit their official website for current hours of operation.

Whether you're attending an event at the convention center, looking for unique Minneapolis souvenirs, or simply want to explore local products, the gift shops at the Minneapolis Convention Center provide a convenient and enjoyable shopping experience.

59.Explore the boutiques in the Uptown neighborhood.

Exploring the boutiques in the Uptown neighborhood of Minneapolis is a trendy and eclectic shopping experience. Here's what you can expect when you visit Uptown's boutiques:

Fashion Boutiques: Uptown is known for its fashionable boutiques that cater to a diverse range of styles and tastes. You can find clothing and accessories for men, women, and children, often featuring both local and national designers.

Independent Designers: Some Uptown boutiques exclusively feature the work of independent and local fashion designers. This is an opportunity to discover unique pieces and support emerging talent.

Vintage and Retro: Uptown boasts several vintage and retro clothing boutiques where you can browse curated selections of vintage clothing, accessories, and footwear from various eras.

Footwear: If you're a shoe enthusiast, you'll find shoe boutiques that offer a wide range of footwear options, from stylish boots and sneakers to unique handmade designs.

Jewelry and Accessories: Uptown boutiques often carry an array of jewelry, handbags, scarves, and other accessories to complement your outfit or make a statement.

Home Decor and Furnishings: Some boutiques in the neighborhood offer home decor items, furniture, and interior design pieces that cater to various design aesthetics.

Artisanal and Handmade Goods: Uptown's boutiques may also showcase artisanal products such as handcrafted candles, ceramics, pottery, and other locally made items.

Local Art: Depending on the boutique, you might find artwork by local artists that reflects the creativity and culture of Minneapolis.

Sustainability: Many Uptown boutiques prioritize sustainability and eco-conscious practices, making them a great destination for eco-friendly and socially responsible shopping.

Community Atmosphere: Uptown's boutique shops often have a friendly and community-oriented atmosphere. Shopkeepers are typically passionate about their products and may offer personalized service and recommendations.

Events and Promotions: Depending on the season and local events, Uptown boutiques may host special events, trunk shows, and promotions that offer discounts and unique shopping experiences.

Accessibility: Uptown is designed to be walkable and accessible to all visitors, including those with disabilities.

Hours: Boutique hours may vary, so it's advisable to check with individual shops or the Uptown neighborhood association for current hours of operation.

Cafes and Eateries: While exploring Uptown's boutiques, you'll also come across charming cafes, eateries, and restaurants where you can take a break, enjoy a meal, or savor a cup of coffee.

Strolling through the boutiques in the Uptown neighborhood allows you to connect with the local fashion scene, discover unique and stylish products, and support independent designers and businesses. Whether you're shopping for clothing, accessories, home decor, or simply enjoying the neighborhood's artistic vibe, Uptown offers a trendy and diverse retail experience in Minneapolis.

60.Hunt for antiques at Hunt & Gather.

Hunting for antiques at Hunt & Gather in Minneapolis is a captivating and nostalgic experience. Here's what you can expect when you visit Hunt & Gather:

Antique Treasures: Hunt & Gather is renowned for its diverse and ever-changing selection of antique and vintage items. You can explore an array of antiques, collectibles, and unique finds from various time periods and styles.

Furniture: The shop often features antique and vintage furniture pieces, including chairs, tables, dressers, cabinets, and more. Whether you're seeking a statement piece or a charming addition to your home, you'll find a range of options.

Home Decor: Hunt & Gather offers a variety of antique home decor items such as mirrors, artwork, lighting fixtures, rugs, and decorative accessories that can add character and history to your living space.

Art and Collectibles: If you're an art enthusiast or collector, you may discover antique paintings, sculptures, ceramics, and other artistic pieces that capture the essence of different eras and artistic movements.

Vintage Clothing and Accessories: The shop may also have a selection of vintage clothing, accessories, and jewelry that reflect the fashion trends of bygone decades.

Kitchenware and Tableware: Vintage kitchenware and tableware items are often available at Hunt & Gather. You can find charming dishes, glassware, utensils, and kitchen gadgets with a vintage flair.

Books and Ephemera: Antique books, magazines, postcards, and other ephemera items are frequently part of the shop's offerings. These items can provide insight into the past and make for intriguing collectibles.

Curiosities and Oddities: Some antique shops, including Hunt & Gather, may feature curiosities and oddities that pique curiosity and spark conversation. These items often have historical or cultural significance.

Friendly Staff: Antique shopkeepers are typically knowledgeable and passionate about the items they curate. They can provide insights into the history and provenance of the antiques and collectibles in the store.

One-of-a-Kind Finds: Antique shopping is like going on a treasure hunt, and each visit to Hunt & Gather may lead to the discovery of unique and one-of-a-kind pieces that hold special meaning.

Community Atmosphere: Antique shops often have a welcoming and community-oriented atmosphere, with fellow shoppers and collectors sharing their enthusiasm for history and nostalgia.

Accessibility: Hunt & Gather is typically designed to be accessible to all visitors, including those with disabilities.

Hours: Antique shop hours may vary, so it's advisable to check Hunt & Gather's website or contact them directly for current hours of operation.

Hunting for antiques at Hunt & Gather is a journey through time, offering a chance to uncover hidden gems, embrace the stories of the past, and acquire timeless pieces that add character and charm to your home. Whether you're a seasoned antique collector or a first-time explorer, Hunt & Gather provides a captivating antique shopping experience in Minneapolis.

61.Picnic in Boom Island Park.

Picnicking in Boom Island Park is a delightful way to enjoy the outdoors, scenic views, and a relaxing meal in Minneapolis. Here's what you can expect when you have a picnic in Boom Island Park:

Natural Beauty: Boom Island Park is situated along the banks of the Mississippi River and offers picturesque views of the water, nearby bridges, and lush greenery. The park's natural beauty provides a serene backdrop for your picnic.

Picnic Areas: The park typically features designated picnic areas equipped with picnic tables, benches, and open spaces where you can spread out a blanket. You can choose a spot that suits your preferences, whether you prefer a shaded area or a sunny spot by the river.

Riverfront Views: One of the highlights of picnicking in Boom Island Park is the opportunity to enjoy riverfront views. You can watch boats go by, observe wildlife, and take in the calming ambiance of the Mississippi River.

Playground: If you're picnicking with children, the park often includes a playground where kids can have fun before or after your meal. It's a great way for families to enjoy their time in the park.

Walking and Biking Trails: Boom Island Park is part of the Grand Rounds Scenic Byway system, and it offers walking and biking trails that allow you to explore the park and the surrounding area on foot or by bicycle.

Fishing: Fishing enthusiasts can bring their gear and try their luck in the Mississippi River. It's a popular spot for anglers looking to catch a variety of fish species.

Birdwatching: The park is home to a variety of bird species, making it a fantastic location for birdwatching. Be sure to bring binoculars if you're interested in observing the local avian residents.

Peaceful Atmosphere: Boom Island Park is known for its peaceful and relaxing atmosphere, making it an ideal place for a quiet picnic or a serene afternoon.

Accessibility: The park is designed to be accessible to all visitors, including those with disabilities. It typically includes accessible pathways and facilities.

Restrooms: Public restrooms are often available within the park for your convenience.

Trash and Recycling: Be sure to clean up after your picnic by disposing of trash and recyclables in the designated receptacles to help keep the park clean.

62. Visit the Eloise Butler Wildflower Garden.

Visiting the Eloise Butler Wildflower Garden in Minneapolis is an opportunity to immerse yourself in a serene and natural oasis. Here's what you can expect when you explore the Eloise Butler Wildflower Garden:

Native Wildflowers: The garden is renowned for its extensive collection of native wildflowers, including a wide variety of species that are indigenous to Minnesota and the Midwest. Depending on the season, you'll encounter vibrant blooms in a kaleidoscope of colors.

Botanical Diversity: In addition to wildflowers, the garden features a diverse range of plants, including trees, shrubs, ferns, grasses, and aquatic plants. The botanical diversity creates a rich and immersive natural experience.

Trails and Pathways: Eloise Butler Wildflower Garden offers well-maintained trails and pathways that wind through the garden's various habitats. These trails allow you to explore different ecosystems, including woodland, wetland, and prairie areas.

Educational Signage: Throughout the garden, you'll find informative signage that provides details about the plants, wildlife, and ecosystems you encounter. These signs offer valuable insights into the natural world.

Birdwatching: The garden is a haven for birdwatchers. It attracts a variety of bird species, making it an excellent spot for observing and listening to the local avian residents.

Butterfly and Pollinator Gardens: Some areas of the garden may be dedicated to butterfly and pollinator-friendly plants, making it an ideal place to observe and learn about these important insects.

Quiet and Peaceful Atmosphere: Eloise Butler Wildflower Garden is known for its tranquility and is an excellent place for nature enthusiasts, photographers, and those seeking a peaceful escape from the city's hustle and bustle.

Picnicking: The garden may offer picnic areas where you can enjoy a meal surrounded by the beauty of nature. Be sure to follow any picnic guidelines or rules established by the garden.

Visitor Center: Depending on the garden's facilities, there may be a visitor center where you can find additional information, maps, and resources about the garden and its offerings.

Accessibility: Efforts are typically made to ensure that the garden is accessible to all visitors, including those with disabilities. Be sure to check with the garden for specific accessibility details.

Conservation and Preservation: The Eloise Butler Wildflower Garden plays a vital role in conserving and preserving native plant species. It often participates in educational and conservation initiatives.

Seasonal Changes: Keep in mind that the garden's appearance and plant life may change with the seasons, so multiple visits throughout the year can provide varying experiences.

Hours: The garden's hours of operation may vary by season, so it's advisable to check the Eloise Butler Wildflower Garden's official website or contact them directly for current hours and any special events or programs.

Visiting the Eloise Butler Wildflower Garden is a chance to connect with the beauty and biodiversity of the natural world. Whether you're a botany enthusiast, a nature lover, or simply seeking a tranquil escape, this garden offers a serene and educational experience in the heart of Minneapolis.

63.Relax in Gold Medal Park.

Relaxing in Gold Medal Park in Minneapolis is a wonderful way to unwind, enjoy outdoor recreation, and take in beautiful urban landscapes. Here's what you can expect when you visit Gold Medal Park:

Scenic Views: Gold Medal Park offers picturesque views of the city's skyline, including the iconic Guthrie Theater and the Mississippi River. It's an ideal spot for capturing stunning photographs of Minneapolis.

Green Space: The park features lush green lawns and manicured landscaping, providing a serene and inviting environment for picnics, leisurely strolls, or simply lounging in the sun.

Public Art: Gold Medal Park is home to several public art installations, including the "Mill City Running Totems" by artists Randy Walker and Mia Kaplan. These artworks add to the park's cultural and aesthetic appeal.

Walking and Biking Trails: The park is connected to the city's extensive network of walking and biking trails, making it a convenient starting point for exploring Minneapolis on foot or by bicycle.

Picnic Areas: Picnic tables and open grassy areas are available for picnicking and relaxation. You can bring your own picnic or grab takeout from nearby restaurants and enjoy an al fresco meal.

Outdoor Activities: The park's open space is perfect for outdoor activities like frisbee, kite flying, or playing catch. Many visitors use the park as a place for exercise and recreation.

Events and Performances: Depending on the season, Gold Medal Park may host community events, outdoor concerts, and cultural performances. These events can add vibrancy and entertainment to your visit.

Accessibility: The park is typically designed to be accessible to all visitors, including those with disabilities. Accessibility features may include accessible pathways and facilities.

Dog-Friendly: Gold Medal Park is often dog-friendly, making it a great place to take your furry companion for a walk. Be sure to follow any posted rules and leash requirements.

Peaceful Atmosphere: Despite its central location, Gold Medal Park offers a peaceful and tranquil atmosphere, making it an oasis in the heart of the city.

Water Features: Some sections of the park may include water features, fountains, or reflecting pools that add to the park's aesthetics and ambiance.

Hours: The park's hours of operation may vary by season, so it's advisable to check the official Gold Medal Park website or contact them directly for current hours and any special events.

Relaxing in Gold Medal Park is a great way to connect with nature, enjoy the cityscape, and unwind in a green and urban setting. Whether you're seeking a quiet escape, outdoor activities, or a place to appreciate art and culture, Gold Medal Park offers a refreshing and inviting space in Minneapolis.

64.Go birdwatching in the Cedar Lake Wildlife Area.

Birdwatching in the Cedar Lake Wildlife Area in Minneapolis is a rewarding and tranquil outdoor activity. Here's what you can expect when you go birdwatching in this natural area:

Travel to Minneapolis Minnesota

Diverse Bird Species: Cedar Lake Wildlife Area is home to a diverse range of bird species. Depending on the season, you may spot waterfowl, songbirds, raptors, and migratory birds. Some common bird sightings include ducks, geese, herons, egrets, warblers, and more.

Natural Habitats: The wildlife area encompasses a variety of natural habitats, including wetlands, woodlands, and shoreline areas along Cedar Lake. These different ecosystems provide a rich and varied environment for birdwatching.

Trails and Observation Points: Cedar Lake Wildlife Area typically features walking trails and observation points that allow birdwatchers to explore the area while keeping a respectful distance from the wildlife. These trails provide opportunities to spot birds in their natural habitat.

Binoculars and Field Guides: Be sure to bring binoculars and field guides to help you identify bird species and learn more about their behaviors, plumage, and vocalizations.

Quiet and Peaceful Environment: Birdwatching in the Cedar Lake Wildlife Area offers a quiet and peaceful environment, perfect for focusing on bird observations, photography, or simply enjoying the serenity of nature.

Seasonal Changes: Keep in mind that bird species can vary depending on the season. Cedar Lake Wildlife Area may be especially vibrant during the spring and fall migrations, but there are birdwatching opportunities year-round.

Birding Etiquette: When birdwatching, it's important to practice ethical birding etiquette. Maintain a respectful distance from the birds, avoid disturbing nests or nesting areas, and carry out any trash or litter to preserve the natural environment.

Accessibility: Depending on the facilities available, the wildlife area may have accessible pathways and viewing areas to accommodate birdwatchers of all abilities.

Hours: The wildlife area's hours of operation may vary, so it's advisable to check with the Cedar Lake Wildlife Area or the Minneapolis Park and Recreation Board for current hours and any special considerations.

Birdwatching in the Cedar Lake Wildlife Area offers an opportunity to connect with nature, learn about local bird species, and appreciate the beauty of the natural world. Whether you're an experienced birder or a beginner, this tranquil setting in Minneapolis provides a serene and enriching birdwatching experience.

65.Play frisbee golf at Bryant Lake Regional Park.

Playing frisbee golf at Bryant Lake Regional Park is a fun and active outdoor experience. Here's what you can expect when you play frisbee golf at this park:

Frisbee Golf Course: Bryant Lake Regional Park typically features a frisbee golf course that includes a series of designated baskets or targets. The course is designed to provide players with a challenging and enjoyable frisbee golf experience.

Rules and Objectives: Frisbee golf, also known as disc golf, follows rules similar to traditional golf. The objective is to complete the course in as few throws as possible, aiming to get your frisbee (disc) into each target (basket) in as few throws as you can.

Equipment: To play frisbee golf, you'll need frisbee golf discs, which are specially designed for different types of throws (drivers, mid-ranges, and putters). You can typically bring your own discs or rent them on-site if available.

Course Layout: The course at Bryant Lake Regional Park is often designed to take advantage of the park's natural terrain, including hills, trees, and open spaces. This provides players with a dynamic and scenic course.

Scoring: Frisbee golf is typically scored based on the number of throws it takes to complete the course. Players aim to complete each hole in as few throws as possible, with the lowest overall score winning.

Variety of Holes: Frisbee golf courses often include a variety of hole types, such as par 3, par 4, and par 5 holes, each with unique challenges and distances.

Family-Friendly: Frisbee golf is a family-friendly activity suitable for all ages and skill levels. It's an excellent way to spend quality time outdoors with friends and family.

Park Amenities: Bryant Lake Regional Park may offer additional amenities such as restrooms, picnic areas, and walking trails, providing opportunities for a full day of outdoor enjoyment.

Accessibility: Depending on the park's facilities, there may be accessible pathways and accommodations for players with disabilities.

Hours: The park's hours of operation and frisbee golf course availability may vary by season, so it's advisable to check with the park's official website or contact them directly for current hours and any special considerations.

Playing frisbee golf at Bryant Lake Regional Park is a recreational and social activity that allows you to enjoy the great outdoors, test your skills, and have fun with friends and fellow players. Whether you're a seasoned disc golfer or new to the game, this park offers an entertaining and challenging course in a scenic setting.

66.Explore the scenic Minnehaha Falls Park.

Exploring Minnehaha Falls Park in Minneapolis is a delightful way to experience natural beauty, hiking trails, and the iconic Minnehaha Falls. Here's what you can expect when you visit Minnehaha Falls Park:

Minnehaha Falls: The park is home to the stunning Minnehaha Falls, a 53-foot (16-meter) waterfall that is one of Minneapolis' most iconic natural attractions. Visitors can admire the rushing cascade and the surrounding rock formations from designated viewing areas.

Scenic Views: Minnehaha Falls Park offers picturesque views of the waterfall, the Minnehaha Creek, and the lush, wooded surroundings. It's a popular spot for photography and taking in the beauty of nature.

Hiking Trails: The park features a network of hiking and walking trails that meander through wooded areas, along the creek, and to various vantage points of the falls. These trails cater to a range of hiking abilities, from leisurely strolls to more challenging hikes.

Historic Structures: Within the park, you may come across historic structures like the Longfellow House, which provides insight into the history of the area and the connection to the famous poet Henry Wadsworth Longfellow.

Biking: Some trails in the park are bike-friendly, allowing cyclists to explore the natural beauty and scenery on two wheels.

Picnicking: Minnehaha Falls Park offers designated picnic areas where you can enjoy a meal or snack surrounded by nature. Be sure to follow any park guidelines for picnicking.

Visitor Center: Depending on the park's facilities, there may be a visitor center or interpretive center where you can learn more about the park's history, geology, and natural features.

Birdwatching: The park's diverse ecosystems make it an excellent location for birdwatching. Bird enthusiasts can spot a variety of avian species in the area.

Accessibility: Efforts are typically made to ensure that the park is accessible to all visitors, including those with disabilities. This may include accessible pathways and facilities.

Wading Pool: In the summer months, there's often a wading pool near the falls where families and children can cool off and play in the water.

Live Music and Events: Depending on the season, the park may host live music performances, cultural events, and community gatherings, providing additional entertainment for visitors.

Dog-Friendly: The park may be dog-friendly, allowing you to bring your furry companion for a walk. Be sure to follow any posted rules and leash requirements.

Hours: Minnehaha Falls Park's hours of operation may vary by season, so it's advisable to check with the Minneapolis Park and Recreation Board or visit the park's official website for current hours and any special events.

Exploring Minnehaha Falls Park is a wonderful way to connect with nature, appreciate the beauty of the waterfall, and enjoy outdoor activities like hiking, picnicking, and birdwatching. Whether you're seeking a leisurely outing or an adventurous hike, this park offers a serene and scenic escape in the heart of Minneapolis.

67.Have a barbecue in Lake Harriet Park.

Having a barbecue in Lake Harriet Park in Minneapolis is a popular and enjoyable outdoor activity. Here's what you can expect when you plan a barbecue at Lake Harriet Park:

Picnic Areas: Lake Harriet Park typically offers designated picnic areas equipped with picnic tables, grills, and open spaces where you can set up your barbecue. These areas are often conveniently located near the shores of Lake Harriet.

Grilling Facilities: The park may provide charcoal or gas grills for public use. Be sure to bring your own charcoal, lighter fluid, and grilling utensils if needed, as these may not always be provided.

Barbecue Grills: Many visitors bring their own portable barbecue grills to the park. Check with the park's guidelines to ensure that personal grills are allowed and follow any safety regulations in place.

Lakeside Views: Lake Harriet Park offers beautiful lakeside views, allowing you to enjoy your barbecue while taking in the serene scenery of Lake Harriet. It's a picturesque setting for outdoor dining.

Picnic Supplies: You can bring your own picnic supplies, including food, beverages, utensils, and seating arrangements. Many visitors pack picnic baskets with a variety of delicious treats.

Recreation: In addition to barbecuing, Lake Harriet Park provides opportunities for various recreational activities such as swimming, fishing, paddleboarding, kayaking, and sailing. It's also a great place for walking, jogging, and biking.

Music and Entertainment: The park often hosts live music performances, including concerts and bandshell events during the summer months. Check the park's event schedule to see if there's any live entertainment happening during your visit.

Restrooms: Public restrooms are typically available within the park for your convenience.

Accessibility: Lake Harriet Park is designed to be accessible to all visitors, including those with disabilities. Accessible pathways and facilities are often provided.

Hours: The park's hours of operation may vary by season, so it's advisable to check with the Minneapolis Park and Recreation Board or visit the park's official website for current hours and any special events or programs.

Permits: Depending on the park's policies, you may need to obtain a permit for group gatherings or large barbecues. Be sure to check the park's regulations and permit requirements in advance.

Barbecuing at Lake Harriet Park is a wonderful way to enjoy a day outdoors with family and friends. Whether you're celebrating a special occasion or simply savoring a leisurely barbecue meal by the lake, this park provides a scenic and inviting setting for your outdoor dining experience in Minneapolis.

68.Take a leisurely walk in Theodore Wirth Regional Park.

Taking a leisurely walk in Theodore Wirth Regional Park in Minneapolis is a peaceful and rejuvenating outdoor activity. Here's what you can expect when you explore this expansive park:

Tranquil Natural Setting: Theodore Wirth Regional Park is one of the largest urban parks in the United States, offering a vast natural landscape with diverse ecosystems, including forests, wetlands, and lakes. It's an ideal place to escape the hustle and bustle of the city and immerse yourself in nature.

Walking Trails: The park features an extensive network of walking and hiking trails that wind through its picturesque terrain. Whether you prefer paved paths or rugged trails, you can find routes suitable for all fitness levels and ages.

Scenic Overlooks: Throughout the park, you'll discover scenic overlooks that provide breathtaking views of the surrounding natural beauty, including the Chain of Lakes, Theodore Wirth Golf Course, and wooded areas.

Picnic Areas: Theodore Wirth Regional Park often includes designated picnic areas where you can enjoy a meal or snack in a peaceful outdoor setting. It's a great spot for a family picnic or a romantic lunch.

Wildlife Viewing: The park is home to a variety of wildlife, including birds, deer, and other animals. Birdwatchers and nature enthusiasts can appreciate the diverse bird species that call the park home.

Winter Activities: In the winter, the park offers opportunities for cross-country skiing, snowshoeing, and snowboarding. There are groomed trails and facilities for winter sports enthusiasts.

Golf: The park is also home to the Theodore Wirth Golf Course, which provides a scenic backdrop for a round of golf in the warmer months.

Accessibility: Efforts are typically made to ensure that the park is accessible to all visitors, including those with disabilities. This includes accessible pathways and facilities.

Peaceful Atmosphere: Theodore Wirth Regional Park offers a tranquil and serene atmosphere, making it a perfect place for a contemplative walk, meditation, or simply enjoying the sounds of nature.

Dog-Friendly: Depending on park regulations, the park may be dog-friendly, allowing you to bring your canine companion for a walk. Be sure to follow any posted rules and leash requirements.

Events and Programs: The park often hosts community events, educational programs, and nature-related activities. Check the park's event calendar for any upcoming programs that align with your interests.

Hours: The park's hours of operation may vary by season, so it's advisable to check with the Minneapolis Park and Recreation Board or visit the park's official website for current hours and any special events or programs.

A leisurely walk in Theodore Wirth Regional Park is an opportunity to connect with nature, enjoy the beauty of the outdoors, and find tranquility within the heart of Minneapolis. Whether you're seeking solitude, exercise, or quality time with loved ones, this expansive park offers a rejuvenating and serene escape.

69. Visit the Lyndale Park Rose Garden.

Visiting the Lyndale Park Rose Garden in Minneapolis is a delightful and fragrant experience. Here's what you can expect when you explore this beautiful garden:

Rose Varieties: Lyndale Park Rose Garden is home to a stunning collection of roses, featuring a wide variety of rose types, colors, and fragrances. You'll find hybrid tea roses, floribunda roses, grandiflora roses, and more. The garden typically showcases over 3,000 rose plants.

Scenic Beauty: The garden's layout is meticulously designed, creating a visually appealing and symmetrical landscape. The manicured lawns, elegant pathways, and vibrant roses make it a picturesque location for photography and leisurely strolls.

Rose Bloom Season: The best time to visit the Lyndale Park Rose Garden is during the peak rose bloom season, which typically occurs in late spring and early summer. This is when the roses are in full bloom, filling the air with their sweet fragrance and creating a vibrant display of colors.

Fragrance and Aesthetics: As you walk through the garden, you'll be enveloped by the sweet scent of roses. The garden's design often includes trellises, pergolas, and other architectural elements that complement the natural beauty of the roses.

Visitor Center: Depending on the park's facilities, there may be a visitor center or information kiosk where you can learn more about the roses, their care, and the history of the garden.

Educational Signage: The garden typically provides informative signage that highlights different rose varieties, their names, and other botanical details. This can enhance your appreciation for these exquisite flowers.

Peaceful Atmosphere: The Lyndale Park Rose Garden offers a peaceful and serene atmosphere, making it a perfect place for quiet reflection, romantic outings, or simply enjoying the beauty of the roses.

Accessibility: Efforts are typically made to ensure that the rose garden is accessible to all visitors, including those with disabilities. This may include accessible pathways and facilities.

Picnicking: While picnicking may not be allowed within the rose garden itself, nearby parks like Lake Harriet Park offer picnic areas where you can enjoy a meal before or after your visit.

Hours: The garden's hours of operation may vary by season, so it's advisable to check with the Minneapolis Park and Recreation Board or visit the garden's official website for current hours and any special events or programs.

The Lyndale Park Rose Garden is a true gem in Minneapolis, offering a sensory-rich experience that combines the visual beauty and sweet fragrance of thousands of roses. Whether you're a dedicated rose enthusiast, a nature lover, or simply seeking a serene and romantic setting, this garden provides a serene and enchanting escape in the heart of the city.

70.Enjoy the views from the Stone Arch Bridge Park.

Enjoying the views from Stone Arch Bridge Park in Minneapolis is a scenic and memorable experience. Here's what you can expect when you visit this iconic location:

Historic Stone Arch Bridge: The centerpiece of the park is the Stone Arch Bridge, a stunning feat of 19th-century engineering. The bridge spans the Mississippi River and offers a unique vantage point for enjoying river views, the Minneapolis skyline, and the picturesque St. Anthony Falls.

Scenic Overlooks: Stone Arch Bridge Park provides several scenic overlooks and viewing platforms that allow you to take in panoramic vistas of the river, the falls, and the surrounding cityscape. These locations are perfect for capturing photographs and admiring the natural and architectural beauty of the area.

Riverfront Stroll: The park features a lovely riverfront walkway that runs along the Mississippi River. You can take a leisurely stroll along this pathway, enjoying the refreshing breeze and the sights and sounds of the river.

Historical Signage: Throughout the park and on the bridge, you'll find informative historical signage that details the bridge's history, its significance, and its role in Minneapolis' development.

Biking and Walking Trails: In addition to the Stone Arch Bridge, the park is often part of the city's extensive network of biking and walking trails. These trails provide opportunities for exploring the riverfront and the city on foot or by bicycle.

Picnic Areas: Depending on the park's facilities, you may find designated picnic areas where you can relax and enjoy a meal while taking in the views.

Accessibility: Efforts are typically made to ensure that the park is accessible to all visitors, including those with disabilities. This includes accessible pathways and facilities.

Peaceful Atmosphere: Stone Arch Bridge Park offers a peaceful and tranquil atmosphere, making it an ideal place for quiet contemplation, relaxation, or simply appreciating the natural and architectural beauty of the area.

Events and Programs: The park occasionally hosts special events, art exhibitions, and community programs, adding to the vibrancy of the area. Check the park's event calendar for any upcoming activities.

Hours: The park's hours of operation may vary by season, so it's advisable to check with the Minneapolis Park and Recreation Board or visit the park's official website for current hours and any special events or programs.

Whether you're interested in history, photography, or simply enjoying a serene stroll with breathtaking views, Stone Arch Bridge Park offers an exceptional location to immerse yourself in the scenic beauty of Minneapolis. The combination of natural splendor and historical significance makes this park a must-visit destination in the city.

71.Explore the Bakken Museum of Electricity.

Exploring the Bakken Museum of Electricity in Minneapolis is a fascinating and educational experience. Here's what you can expect when you visit this unique museum:

History of Electricity: The Bakken Museum is dedicated to the history and science of electricity and magnetism. It provides insights into the development of these fundamental forces, their applications, and their impact on technology and society.

Exhibits: The museum features a wide range of interactive exhibits and displays that explore the principles of electricity and magnetism. These exhibits often include hands-on activities and demonstrations that allow visitors to experiment and learn.

Historical Artifacts: The Bakken Museum houses a remarkable collection of historical artifacts related to electricity and magnetism. You can expect to see early electrical devices, vintage medical equipment, and scientific instruments from various time periods.

Medicine and Electricity: One of the museum's unique focuses is the relationship between electricity and medicine. It showcases the historical use of electricity in medical treatments and research, offering insights into the evolution of medical technology.

Outdoor Space: In addition to indoor exhibits, the museum may have outdoor spaces and gardens that feature sculptures, art installations, and interactive displays related to electricity and natural phenomena.

Educational Programs: The Bakken Museum often offers educational programs, workshops, and events for visitors of all ages. These programs can include science demonstrations, lectures, and hands-on activities that make learning about electricity engaging and fun.

Historical Context: The museum provides historical context to the development of electricity, highlighting key inventors, scientists, and engineers who contributed to our understanding of this vital force.

Accessibility: Efforts are typically made to ensure that the museum is accessible to all visitors, including those with disabilities. This includes accessible pathways and facilities.

Visitor Center: Depending on the museum's facilities, there may be a visitor center or information desk where you can obtain maps, brochures, and additional information about the exhibits and programs.

Gift Shop: Many museums have gift shops where you can purchase educational books, science-themed gifts, and souvenirs related to electricity and magnetism.

Hours: The museum's hours of operation may vary by season and day of the week, so it's advisable to check with the Bakken Museum's official website or contact them directly for current hours, admission fees, and any special events or exhibitions.

The Bakken Museum of Electricity offers a unique opportunity to explore the fascinating world of electricity, from its historical origins to its modern applications. Whether you're a science enthusiast, a history buff, or a curious learner of any age, this museum provides an engaging and enlightening experience in the heart of Minneapolis.

72. Visit the Bell Museum of Natural History.

Visiting the Bell Museum of Natural History in Minneapolis is an enriching and educational experience. Here's what you can expect when you explore this renowned museum:

Natural History Exhibits: The Bell Museum is dedicated to the natural world and typically features a diverse range of exhibits that showcase the wonders of biology, geology, astronomy, and anthropology. These exhibits often include dioramas, specimens, interactive displays, and informative signage.

Minnesota's Natural Heritage: The museum often highlights Minnesota's unique natural heritage, including its flora, fauna, and ecosystems. You can expect to learn about the state's diverse habitats, wildlife, and geological features.

Planetarium: The Bell Museum typically houses a state-of-the-art planetarium, offering immersive astronomy experiences. Visitors can enjoy planetarium shows, stargazing events, and educational programs that explore the cosmos.

Hands-On Learning: Many exhibits at the museum are interactive, allowing visitors to engage in hands-on learning and exploration. This interactive approach makes science and natural history accessible and engaging for all ages.

Educational Programs: The Bell Museum often hosts educational programs, workshops, lectures, and special events that cater to a wide range of interests and ages. These programs provide deeper insights into natural history and science.

Diverse Collections: The museum houses extensive collections of natural specimens, including fossils, minerals, plants, and animal specimens. These collections are valuable resources for research and education.

Accessibility: The Bell Museum typically strives to ensure that its facilities are accessible to all visitors, including those with disabilities. This includes accessible pathways, exhibits, and facilities.

Visitor Center: Depending on the museum's facilities, there may be a visitor center or information desk where you can obtain maps, brochures, and additional information about the exhibits and programs.

Gift Shop: Many museums have gift shops where you can purchase educational books, science-themed gifts, and souvenirs related to natural history and astronomy.

Café or Dining Options: The museum may offer on-site dining options or a café where you can enjoy a meal or refreshments during your visit.

Hours: The museum's hours of operation may vary by season and day of the week, so it's advisable to check with the Bell Museum's official website or contact them directly for current hours, admission fees, and any special events or exhibitions.

The Bell Museum of Natural History provides an opportunity to explore and appreciate the natural world, from the depths of Earth's history to the vastness of the cosmos. Whether you're a science enthusiast, a nature lover, or simply seeking an educational and engaging experience, this museum offers a captivating journey through the wonders of the natural sciences in Minneapolis.

73.Discover the Raptor Center at the University of Minnesota.

Discovering the Raptor Center at the University of Minnesota in St. Paul is an opportunity to get up close and personal with these magnificent birds of prey and learn about their conservation. Here's what you can expect when you visit:

Raptor Rehabilitation: The Raptor Center specializes in the rescue, rehabilitation, and release of injured and orphaned raptors. During your visit, you may have the chance to observe the center's dedicated staff and volunteers caring for these birds and treating their injuries.

Raptor Education: The center offers educational programs and exhibits that focus on the biology, behavior, and conservation of raptors. You'll learn about the different species of raptors, their unique adaptations, and their roles in ecosystems.

Live Raptor Encounters: One of the highlights of visiting the Raptor Center is the opportunity to see live raptors up close. The center typically houses several permanent resident birds that are used for educational purposes. These birds include eagles, hawks, owls, and falcons.

Guided Tours: Guided tours are often available to provide visitors with in-depth information about the center's work, the raptors in residence, and the importance of raptor conservation.

Visitor Center: Depending on the center's facilities, there may be a visitor center with interactive exhibits, educational displays, and information about the center's mission and programs.

Gift Shop: Many wildlife centers have gift shops where you can purchase souvenirs, educational materials, and items related to raptors and conservation.

Educational Programs: The Raptor Center frequently offers educational programs, workshops, and events for visitors of all ages. These programs can include raptor releases, expert talks, and opportunities for hands-on learning.

Accessibility: Efforts are typically made to ensure that the Raptor Center is accessible to all visitors, including those with disabilities. This includes accessible pathways, exhibits, and facilities.

Hours: The center's hours of operation may vary, so it's advisable to check with the Raptor Center's official website or contact them directly for current hours, admission fees, and any special events or programs.

The Raptor Center at the University of Minnesota provides a unique and engaging experience for nature enthusiasts and those interested in wildlife conservation. It's a place where you can gain a deeper understanding of raptors, their importance in ecosystems, and the efforts being made to protect and rehabilitate these remarkable birds.

74.Take a riverboat cruise on the Mississippi River.

Taking a riverboat cruise on the Mississippi River in Minneapolis is a delightful way to experience the scenic beauty and history of the river. Here's what you can expect when you embark on such a cruise:

Scenic Views: Riverboat cruises typically offer passengers panoramic views of the Mississippi River and its surroundings. You'll have the opportunity to admire the natural beauty of the riverbanks, including lush forests, wildlife, and serene waters.

Historical Narration: Many riverboat cruises provide informative narration or guided commentary about the history, culture, and significance of the Mississippi River. You'll learn about the river's role in trade, transportation, and the development of the region.

Sightseeing: Riverboat cruises often pass by notable landmarks and points of interest along the river, such as historic bridges, downtown Minneapolis, and scenic bluffs. It's a great way to see the city from a unique vantage point.

Live Entertainment: Some riverboat cruises may feature live entertainment on board, including music, performances, or themed events. Check with the cruise operator to see if any special entertainment is offered during your cruise.

Refreshments: Depending on the cruise, there may be options for onboard dining or refreshments. You can often enjoy a meal, snacks, or beverages while taking in the river views.

Special Cruises: Throughout the year, riverboat operators may offer special cruises for holidays, seasonal events, or themed experiences. These can include sunset cruises, fall foliage tours, and more.

Accessibility: Efforts are typically made to ensure that riverboat cruises are accessible to all passengers, including those with disabilities. Be sure to check with the cruise operator about accessibility options.

Seasonal Availability: Riverboat cruises may operate seasonally, with schedules varying depending on weather conditions and river conditions. It's advisable to check with the specific cruise company for their operating dates and times.

Ticketing: Tickets for riverboat cruises can typically be purchased in advance online or on-site at the dock. Be sure to book your tickets in advance, especially during peak tourist seasons.

Duration: The length of riverboat cruises can vary, with options for shorter sightseeing tours and longer excursions. Check with the cruise operator for details on the duration of your chosen cruise.

A riverboat cruise on the Mississippi River offers a relaxing and informative way to connect with nature, history, and the city of Minneapolis. Whether you're interested in sightseeing, learning about local history, or simply enjoying a peaceful journey on the water, a riverboat cruise is a memorable experience in the heart of the Twin Cities.

75.Explore the Science Museum of Minneapolis in St. Paul.

Exploring the Science Museum of Minnesota in St. Paul is an engaging and educational experience for visitors of all ages. Here's what you can expect when you visit this dynamic museum:

Hands-On Exhibits: The Science Museum of Minnesota features a wide array of interactive and hands-on exhibits that explore various aspects of science, technology, engineering, and mathematics (STEM). These exhibits often encourage active learning, experimentation, and discovery.

Omni-Theater: The museum typically includes an Omni-Theater, which is an immersive giant screen theater offering breathtaking films on a variety of scientific and natural subjects. It provides a unique cinematic experience with its massive screen and state-of-the-art technology.

Dinosaur and Fossil Displays: A highlight of the museum is its extensive collection of dinosaur fossils and exhibits related to paleontology. You can expect to see life-sized dinosaur models, fossils, and information about prehistoric life.

Human Body Gallery: The museum often features exhibits that explore the human body, health, and biology. These exhibits may include interactive displays, anatomical models, and information about human health and wellness.

Science Live! Performances: Visitors can typically enjoy live science demonstrations, performances, and experiments conducted by museum educators and experts. These entertaining and informative shows enhance the learning experience.

Temporary Exhibitions: The museum frequently hosts temporary exhibitions that cover a wide range of scientific topics, from space exploration to environmental sustainability. These exhibitions provide fresh and engaging content for return visitors.

Educational Programs: The Science Museum of Minnesota offers educational programs, workshops, and events for visitors of all ages. These programs often cater to students, families, and educators, providing opportunities for deeper learning and exploration.

Accessibility: Efforts are typically made to ensure that the museum is accessible to all visitors, including those with disabilities. This includes accessible pathways, exhibits, and facilities.

Visitor Center and Gift Shop: The museum typically has a visitor center or information desk where you can obtain maps, brochures, and additional information about exhibits and programs. The gift shop offers science-themed merchandise, books, and educational toys.

Café or Dining Options: Depending on the museum's facilities, there may be on-site dining options or a café where you can enjoy a meal or refreshments during your visit.

Hours and Tickets: The museum's hours of operation, admission fees, and ticketing information may vary, so it's advisable to check with the Science Museum of Minnesota's official website or contact them directly for current hours and any special events or exhibitions.

The Science Museum of Minnesota provides an exciting and immersive journey into the world of science, technology, and natural history. Whether you're interested in space exploration, paleontology, or the wonders of the human body, this museum offers an enriching and entertaining experience in the heart of St. Paul.

76.Go stargazing at the Minneapolis Planetarium.

Stargazing at the Minneapolis Planetarium is a captivating experience for anyone interested in astronomy and celestial wonders. Here's what you can expect when you visit:

Astronomy Shows: The Minneapolis Planetarium typically offers a variety of astronomy shows and planetarium presentations. These immersive shows use a planetarium dome to simulate the night sky, providing a detailed and educational journey through the cosmos.

Planetarium Exhibits: In addition to shows, the planetarium may feature interactive exhibits related to astronomy and space science. These exhibits often allow visitors to explore celestial phenomena, the solar system, and the universe's mysteries.

Educational Programs: The planetarium often hosts educational programs, workshops, and events that cater to astronomy enthusiasts, students, and the general public. These programs can include lectures, star parties, and hands-on activities related to space and astronomy.

Public Observing Nights: Depending on the planetarium's facilities, it may offer public observing nights where visitors can use telescopes to view celestial objects like planets, stars, and galaxies. These events are typically led by knowledgeable astronomers.

Stargazing Tips: The planetarium staff may provide stargazing tips, information on celestial events, and guidance on how to observe the night sky from your own backyard.

Accessibility: Efforts are typically made to ensure that the planetarium is accessible to all visitors, including those with disabilities. This may include accessible facilities and accommodations.

Visitor Center and Gift Shop: The planetarium often has a visitor center or information desk where you can obtain maps, brochures, and additional information about shows and programs. You may also find a gift shop offering astronomy-related merchandise and educational materials.

Hours and Tickets: The planetarium's hours of operation, admission fees, and ticketing information may vary based on show schedules and special events. Be sure to check with the Minneapolis Planetarium's official website or contact them directly for current hours and upcoming shows.

Stargazing at the Minneapolis Planetarium provides a unique opportunity to explore the cosmos, learn about the mysteries of the universe, and gain a deeper appreciation for the beauty of the night sky. Whether you're a seasoned astronomer or a curious beginner, the planetarium offers a captivating journey through the wonders of the universe.

77. Visit the Minnesota Zoo in nearby Apple Valley.

Visiting the Minnesota Zoo in Apple Valley is a fantastic way to connect with wildlife, explore diverse ecosystems, and enjoy educational and entertaining exhibits. Here's what you can expect when you visit:

Animal Exhibits: The Minnesota Zoo is home to a wide variety of animals from around the world. You can explore exhibits that feature mammals, birds, reptiles, amphibians, and fish. These exhibits are designed to replicate the animals' natural habitats, providing a close and immersive experience.

Educational Opportunities: The zoo offers numerous educational programs and opportunities for visitors of all ages. These can include animal demonstrations, keeper talks, and interactive displays that teach visitors about wildlife conservation, ecology, and biology.

Conservation Efforts: The Minnesota Zoo is committed to wildlife conservation and often collaborates with conservation organizations to protect endangered species. You can learn about the zoo's conservation initiatives and how they contribute to the preservation of animal species and their habitats.

Outdoor and Indoor Exhibits: Depending on the weather and the season, you can explore both outdoor and indoor exhibits. The indoor exhibits are particularly enjoyable during colder months or inclement weather.

Special Exhibits: The zoo frequently hosts special and rotating exhibits that focus on specific animal species or themes. These exhibits offer fresh and exciting experiences for return visitors.

Accessibility: Efforts are made to ensure that the zoo is accessible to all visitors, including those with disabilities. This includes accessible pathways, exhibits, and facilities.

Visitor Center and Gift Shop: The zoo typically has a visitor center or information desk where you can obtain maps, brochures, and additional information about the exhibits and programs. You can also visit the gift shop for souvenirs, animal-themed merchandise, and educational materials.

Cafes and Dining Options: You'll find cafes and dining options within the zoo where you can enjoy a meal or refreshments during your visit.

Hours and Tickets: The zoo's hours of operation, admission fees, and ticketing information may vary based on the season and special events. It's advisable to check with the Minnesota Zoo's official website or contact them directly for current hours, ticket prices, and any upcoming events or exhibitions.

The Minnesota Zoo offers a wonderful opportunity to learn about wildlife from around the globe, appreciate the importance of conservation, and have an enjoyable day surrounded by animals and nature. Whether you're visiting with family, friends, or on your own, the zoo provides a memorable and enriching experience in the Twin Cities area.

78. Learn about marine life at SEA LIFE at Mall of America.

Exploring SEA LIFE at Mall of America is a captivating way to delve into the fascinating world of marine life. Here's what you can expect when you visit this unique aquarium:

Marine Exhibits: SEA LIFE showcases a diverse array of marine creatures and ecosystems. You'll encounter a wide variety of aquatic species, including tropical fish, seahorses, rays, sharks, and even sea turtles. The exhibits are designed to replicate the natural habitats of these creatures, allowing you to observe them up close.

Interactive Touch Pools: Many visitors' favorite experiences at SEA LIFE are the interactive touch pools. Here, you can get hands-on with creatures like starfish and sea anemones, providing a tactile and educational encounter with marine life.

Educational Presentations: The aquarium typically offers scheduled educational presentations and talks by knowledgeable staff and marine experts. These presentations cover topics such as marine conservation, animal behavior, and the importance of protecting ocean ecosystems.

Conservation Initiatives: SEA LIFE is often involved in marine conservation efforts. You can learn about the aquarium's conservation initiatives and how they contribute to the protection of marine species and their habitats.

Underwater Tunnel: One of the highlights of SEA LIFE is its underwater tunnel. This tunnel allows you to walk through a transparent corridor surrounded by water, providing the sensation of being submerged in an ocean environment. You'll have the chance to see sharks, rays, and other marine creatures swimming above and around you.

Accessibility: Efforts are typically made to ensure that SEA LIFE is accessible to all visitors, including those with disabilities. This includes accessible pathways and facilities.

Visitor Center and Gift Shop: The aquarium often has a visitor center or information desk where you can obtain maps, brochures, and additional information about the exhibits and programs. You can also explore the gift shop for marine-themed merchandise, souvenirs, and educational materials.

Café and Dining Options: Depending on the facilities, you may find a café or dining options within the aquarium where you can enjoy refreshments during your visit.

Hours and Tickets: SEA LIFE's hours of operation and admission fees may vary by season and special events. It's advisable to check with SEA LIFE at Mall of America's official website or contact them directly for current hours, ticket prices, and any upcoming events or exhibitions.

SEA LIFE at Mall of America offers an immersive and educational journey through the mysteries of the deep blue sea. Whether you're a marine enthusiast, a family looking for an exciting outing, or someone simply interested in the wonders of the ocean, this aquarium provides an enriching and entertaining experience in the heart of Minnesota.

79.Attend a nature program at Eloise Butler Wildflower Garden.

Attending a nature program at Eloise Butler Wildflower Garden is a wonderful way to connect with nature and deepen your understanding of native plants and ecosystems. Here's what you can expect when you participate in one of their programs:

Educational Programs: Eloise Butler Wildflower Garden typically offers a variety of educational programs throughout the year. These programs are designed to teach visitors about the unique plants, wildlife, and habitats found within the garden and its surrounding natural areas.

Guided Tours: Nature programs often include guided tours led by knowledgeable naturalists and experts. These tours provide insights into the garden's history, the native plants and wildflowers, and the ecological significance of the area.

Wildflower Walks: Eloise Butler Wildflower Garden is renowned for its diverse collection of native wildflowers. Nature programs may include wildflower walks where you can learn about the different species, their blooming seasons, and their ecological roles.

Bird Watching: The garden is also a great spot for birdwatching. Nature programs may include birdwatching sessions where you can observe and learn about the various bird species that inhabit the area.

Insect and Pollinator Programs: Eloise Butler Wildflower Garden is home to a variety of insects and pollinators. Some programs may focus on the important role of these creatures in native plant ecosystems.

Photography and Art Workshops: For those interested in capturing the beauty of the garden, photography and art workshops may be offered. These workshops provide tips and techniques for capturing the natural beauty of the area.

Hands-On Activities: Many nature programs incorporate hands-on activities, such as plant identification, nature journaling, or seed collection.

Accessibility: The garden typically strives to ensure that its programs are accessible to all participants, including those with disabilities. Be sure to check with Eloise Butler Wildflower Garden for information on accessibility options.

Visitor Center: Depending on the garden's facilities, there may be a visitor center or information desk where you can obtain maps, brochures, and additional information about programs and events.

Hours and Registration: Nature program schedules, registration requirements, and fees may vary, so it's advisable to check with Eloise Butler Wildflower Garden's official website or contact them directly for current program listings, schedules, and registration details.

Participating in a nature program at Eloise Butler Wildflower Garden offers an opportunity to immerse yourself in the natural beauty of Minnesota, learn about native plants and wildlife, and gain a deeper appreciation for the natural world. Whether you're a nature enthusiast, a budding naturalist, or simply looking for an enriching outdoor experience, these programs provide a rewarding connection to the natural environment.

80.Explore the Mississippi National River and Recreation Area.

Exploring the Mississippi National River and Recreation Area is a fantastic way to connect with nature, history, and outdoor activities along the Mississippi River. Here's what you can expect when you visit this scenic and diverse area:

Scenic Beauty: The Mississippi National River and Recreation Area offer stunning views of the Mississippi River and its surrounding landscapes. Whether you're hiking, biking, or simply enjoying a leisurely stroll along the riverbanks, you'll be treated to beautiful natural vistas.

Outdoor Activities: The recreation area provides ample opportunities for outdoor activities. You can hike scenic trails, go birdwatching, have a picnic, or enjoy water-based activities like kayaking, fishing, and boating. There are often designated areas for these activities, so be sure to check regulations and safety guidelines.

Historical Sites: The Mississippi River has played a significant role in American history, and the recreation area includes historical sites and interpretive centers that showcase the river's importance. You may have the chance to explore historic buildings, learn about the river's past, and gain insights into the people and events that shaped the region.

Wildlife Viewing: The area is home to a variety of wildlife, including eagles, herons, beavers, and more. Bring your binoculars, and you might spot some of these creatures in their natural habitats.

Visitor Centers: Depending on the specific location within the recreation area, there may be visitor centers where you can obtain maps, brochures, and information about the area's natural and cultural resources. These centers often provide exhibits and educational materials.

Educational Programs: The recreation area typically offers educational programs, guided tours, and ranger-led activities that enhance the visitor experience. These programs may cover topics such as ecology, geology, and history.

Accessibility: Efforts are made to ensure that the recreation area is accessible to all visitors, including those with disabilities. This includes accessible trails, facilities, and interpretive materials.

Seasonal Activities: Activities and accessibility may vary by season. Some areas may offer winter activities such as cross-country skiing and snowshoeing when weather conditions permit.

Fees: Many parts of the recreation area are free to visit, but some locations may have entrance fees or require parking passes. It's a good idea to check with the specific sites within the recreation area for any applicable fees.

Hours: The hours of operation for visitor centers, trails, and facilities may vary by location and season. Be sure to check with the specific sites or the Mississippi National River and Recreation Area's official website for current hours and any special events.

Exploring the Mississippi National River and Recreation Area allows you to experience the natural beauty and cultural heritage of the Mississippi River in the heart of the Twin Cities. Whether you're an outdoor enthusiast, a history buff, or simply seeking a peaceful escape into nature, this scenic area offers a wide range of activities and experiences for all ages.

81. Visit the Minnesota Children's Museum in St. Paul.

Visiting the Minnesota Children's Museum in St. Paul is an exciting and educational experience for families and young learners. Here's what you can expect when you visit this engaging museum:

Interactive Exhibits: The Minnesota Children's Museum is known for its hands-on and interactive exhibits that are designed to spark creativity, curiosity, and learning in children of all ages. These exhibits often cover a wide range of topics, including science, art, culture, and more.

Art and Creativity: Many exhibits at the museum focus on art and creativity, allowing children to explore their artistic talents through activities like painting, sculpture, and imaginative play. These spaces often encourage self-expression and experimentation.

Science and Discovery: Science-themed exhibits often feature interactive experiments, puzzles, and activities that introduce children to concepts in physics, biology, engineering, and more. Kids can learn through play and exploration.

Cultural Exploration: Some exhibits provide opportunities for children to learn about different cultures, traditions, and global perspectives. These exhibits may include elements of world geography, history, and multiculturalism.

Early Childhood Play: The museum often includes dedicated areas for younger children, such as toddlers and preschoolers, where age-appropriate activities and play spaces are designed to promote early childhood development.

Educational Programs: The museum offers a variety of educational programs, workshops, and events that enhance the learning experience. These programs may include science demonstrations, storytelling sessions, and art workshops.

Accessibility: Efforts are typically made to ensure that the museum is accessible to all visitors, including those with disabilities. This includes accessible play areas and facilities.

Visitor Services: The museum usually provides visitor services, including a visitor center or information desk where you can obtain maps, brochures, and details about exhibits and programs. There may also be a gift shop offering educational toys and games.

Café or Dining Options: Depending on the museum's facilities, you may find a café or dining options where you can enjoy a meal or snacks during your visit.

Membership: The museum often offers membership programs that provide benefits like unlimited access, discounts on programs and events, and exclusive member-only hours.

Hours and Admission: The museum's hours of operation, admission fees, and ticketing information may vary, so it's advisable to check with the Minnesota Children's Museum's official website or contact them directly for current hours and any special events or exhibitions.

The Minnesota Children's Museum provides a stimulating and interactive environment where children can learn through play and exploration. It's a place where families can spend quality time together, and young minds can thrive in an environment that encourages curiosity and discovery.

82.Explore the Como Park Zoo and Conservatory.

Exploring the Como Park Zoo and Conservatory in St. Paul is a delightful experience that combines the wonders of a zoo with the beauty of botanical gardens. Here's what you can expect when you visit this popular attraction:

Zoo Exhibits: Como Park Zoo is home to a diverse collection of animals from around the world. You can expect to see animals such as lions, giraffes, zebras, gorillas, and many more. The zoo is designed to provide animals with naturalistic habitats that mimic their native environments, offering visitors an immersive and educational experience.

Conservation Initiatives: Many modern zoos, including Como Park, are actively involved in conservation efforts. You can learn about the zoo's initiatives to protect endangered species and their natural habitats, as well as their commitment to global conservation efforts.

Botanical Gardens: The Como Park Conservatory is a highlight of the attraction, featuring a stunning collection of indoor gardens with a wide variety of exotic and tropical plants. The conservatory provides a lush and serene environment for visitors to explore.

Educational Programs: Como Park offers educational programs, workshops, and events for visitors of all ages. These programs often include animal demonstrations, educational talks, and opportunities to learn about wildlife conservation and plant biology.

Special Exhibits: The zoo and conservatory frequently host special and seasonal exhibits that focus on specific themes or species. These exhibits offer fresh and exciting experiences for return visitors.

Accessibility: Efforts are typically made to ensure that Como Park is accessible to all visitors, including those with disabilities. This includes accessible pathways, exhibits, and facilities.

Visitor Center and Gift Shop: You can usually find a visitor center or information desk where you can obtain maps, brochures, and additional information about the zoo and conservatory. The gift shop offers souvenirs, animal-themed merchandise, and educational materials.

Café and Dining Options: Depending on the facilities, there may be on-site dining options or a café where you can enjoy a meal or refreshments during your visit.

Hours and Tickets: The zoo and conservatory have specific hours of operation and admission fees, which may vary by season and age group. Be sure to check with Como Park Zoo and Conservatory's official website or contact them directly for current hours, ticket prices, and any upcoming events or exhibitions.

Como Park Zoo and Conservatory is a perfect destination for families, nature enthusiasts, and anyone looking to escape into a world of animals and botanical beauty. It offers a combination of educational experiences, wildlife conservation efforts, and the chance to connect with the natural world in a lush and inviting setting.

83.Enjoy a day at Valleyfair amusement park.

Valleyfair amusement park is a popular destination for thrill-seekers and families alike, offering a wide range of rides, attractions, and entertainment options. Here's what you can expect when you spend a day at Valleyfair:

Thrilling Rides: Valleyfair is known for its exciting and thrilling rides, including roller coasters, water rides, and thrill rides that cater to adrenaline junkies. Whether you're a fan of high-speed coasters or classic amusement park attractions, you'll find rides that suit your preferences.

Family-Friendly Attractions: In addition to thrill rides, Valleyfair offers a variety of family-friendly attractions, such as carousels, bumper cars, and gentle rides suitable for all ages. It's a great place for families to enjoy quality time together.

Water Park: Valleyfair includes a water park called Soak City, which features water slides, wave pools, lazy rivers, and splash areas. It's the perfect place to cool off on a hot day and enjoy aquatic fun.

Live Entertainment: The park often hosts live entertainment shows, performances, and special events throughout the season. Check the park's schedule for details on shows, concerts, and character meet-and-greets.

Dining Options: Valleyfair offers a variety of dining options, from quick-service eateries to sit-down restaurants. You can enjoy a range of food, snacks, and beverages to refuel during your visit.

Games and Midway Attractions: Test your skills at a variety of carnival-style games and midway attractions, where you can win prizes and have fun competing with friends and family.

Special Events: Valleyfair frequently hosts special events and seasonal celebrations, including Halloween-themed events, holiday festivities, and more. Be sure to check the park's calendar for any upcoming events during your visit.

Accessibility: The park is designed to be accessible to guests with disabilities, including accessible pathways, facilities, and services.

Visitor Services: You'll typically find visitor services like information desks and guest relations offices where you can obtain park maps, information about ride restrictions, and assistance with any questions or concerns.

Souvenirs and Merchandise: Valleyfair has gift shops and souvenir stands throughout the park where you can purchase park memorabilia, clothing, and other merchandise.

Hours and Tickets: The park's hours of operation, admission fees, and ticketing options may vary based on the season and any special events. Be sure to check Valleyfair's official website or contact them directly for current hours and ticket prices.

Valleyfair amusement park provides a full day of entertainment, excitement, and fun for visitors of all ages. Whether you're looking for heart-pounding thrills, family-friendly attractions, or a water park adventure, Valleyfair has something for everyone to enjoy.

84.Go indoor rock climbing at Vertical Endeavors.

Indoor rock climbing at Vertical Endeavors is a thrilling and physically challenging experience for climbers of all skill levels. Here's what you can expect when you visit one of their climbing facilities:

Climbing Walls: Vertical Endeavors boasts a variety of climbing walls that cater to climbers of different abilities, from beginners to advanced climbers. These walls are designed to simulate natural rock features and provide a safe and controlled environment for climbing.

Bouldering: Bouldering is a form of climbing without ropes, typically done on shorter walls with crash pads below for protection. Vertical Endeavors often has dedicated bouldering areas where climbers can test their strength and problem-solving skills.

Routes for All Levels: The climbing walls are typically color-coded to indicate different routes of varying difficulty levels. This allows climbers to choose routes that match their skill and experience, providing a sense of accomplishment as they progress.

Equipment Rental: If you're new to climbing, Vertical Endeavors typically offers equipment rental services, including climbing shoes and harnesses. You'll also receive safety instructions and guidance from the staff.

Safety Measures: Safety is a top priority in indoor climbing gyms. Before climbing, participants often receive a safety briefing and are taught how to use climbing equipment properly. Belaying systems, which provide protection when climbing with ropes, are used to ensure safety.

Instruction and Classes: Many climbing gyms, including Vertical Endeavors, offer instructional classes and clinics for climbers looking to improve their skills. These classes may cover topics such as technique, lead climbing, and outdoor climbing skills.

Youth Programs: Climbing gyms often have youth programs and climbing teams for kids and teenagers interested in learning to climb or improving their climbing abilities.

Fitness Facilities: Some climbing gyms, including Vertical Endeavors, may have fitness facilities on-site, including weightlifting and cardio equipment. This allows climbers to complement their climbing workouts with strength and conditioning training.

Climbing Community: Indoor climbing gyms foster a sense of community among climbers. You'll often find a diverse group of climbers sharing their passion for the sport, and it's a great place to meet like-minded individuals.

Events and Competitions: Climbing gyms may host climbing events, competitions, and social gatherings throughout the year. These events provide opportunities to challenge yourself, meet other climbers, and have fun.

Accessibility: Efforts are typically made to ensure that climbing gyms are accessible to climbers of all abilities and physical conditions.

Hours and Memberships: Vertical Endeavors' hours of operation and membership options may vary by location. Be sure to check with the specific facility you plan to visit for current hours and membership details.

Indoor rock climbing at Vertical Endeavors offers a fantastic way to stay active, challenge yourself both physically and mentally, and enjoy the camaraderie of the climbing community. Whether you're a seasoned climber or a beginner looking to try something new, it's an exhilarating adventure worth experiencing.

85. Visit the Science Museum of Minnesota.

Visiting the Science Museum of Minnesota in St. Paul is an enriching and educational experience for individuals, families, and science enthusiasts. Here's what you can expect when you explore this captivating museum:

Interactive Exhibits: The Science Museum of Minnesota features a wide range of interactive and hands-on exhibits that cover diverse scientific disciplines. These exhibits often explore topics such as biology, physics, earth sciences, technology, and more. Visitors can engage with exhibits, conduct experiments, and learn through interactive displays.

Omni-Theater: The museum often includes an Omni-Theater, where you can watch immersive films on a giant domed screen. These films cover various scientific subjects and provide a unique cinematic experience.

Dinosaurs and Fossils: Many science museums have extensive collections of dinosaur fossils and prehistoric specimens. The Science Museum of Minnesota typically has impressive dinosaur exhibits, showcasing the history and evolution of these ancient creatures.

Live Demonstrations: Throughout the museum, you may encounter live demonstrations and science experiments conducted by museum educators and experts. These demonstrations offer insights into scientific concepts and principles.

Permanent and Rotating Exhibits: In addition to permanent exhibits, the museum often hosts rotating exhibitions that focus on specific scientific topics, historical events, or cultural phenomena. These exhibitions provide fresh and exciting content for repeat visitors.

Educational Programs: The museum offers a variety of educational programs and workshops for visitors of all ages. These programs may include science classes, camps, and special events designed to enhance learning and engagement.

Accessibility: Efforts are made to ensure that the museum is accessible to all visitors, including those with disabilities. This includes accessible pathways, facilities, and accommodations.

Visitor Services: You'll typically find visitor services such as information desks and guest relations offices where you can obtain maps, brochures, and details about exhibits and programs.

Gift Shop: Most museums have a gift shop where you can purchase science-related merchandise, educational toys, books, and souvenirs.

Café and Dining Options: Depending on the facilities, you may find a café or dining options where you can enjoy a meal or snacks during your visit.

Hours and Tickets: The museum's hours of operation, admission fees, and ticketing options may vary based on the season and any special events. Be sure to check the Science Museum of Minnesota's official website or contact them directly for current hours, ticket prices, and any upcoming events or exhibitions.

The Science Museum of Minnesota offers an exciting opportunity to explore the wonders of science, technology, and the natural world. It's a place where curiosity is encouraged, and visitors can embark on a journey of discovery and learning. Whether you're passionate about science or simply looking for an educational and entertaining experience, this museum has something for everyone to enjoy.

86.Have a family picnic in Minnehaha Regional Park.

Having a family picnic in Minnehaha Regional Park is a delightful way to enjoy the natural beauty and outdoor amenities that this Minneapolis park has to offer. Here's what you can expect when you plan a picnic in this scenic park:

Scenic Setting: Minnehaha Regional Park is renowned for its picturesque beauty, featuring a stunning 53-foot waterfall, lush greenery, and scenic river views. You'll find numerous scenic spots where you can set up your picnic and enjoy the natural surroundings.

Picnic Areas: The park typically has designated picnic areas equipped with picnic tables, benches, and trash receptacles. These areas provide a comfortable and convenient space for picnicking with your family.

River Views: The park is situated along the banks of the Mississippi River, offering opportunities for picnickers to enjoy river views and watch boats passing by. The sound of rushing water from Minnehaha Falls adds to the tranquil atmosphere.

Waterfall Viewing: Be sure to visit Minnehaha Falls, the park's centerpiece. A short walk from the picnic areas, the falls are a popular attraction where you can take in the natural beauty of the cascading water.

Walking Trails: Minnehaha Regional Park features walking and hiking trails that wind through the park's wooded areas and along the river. After your picnic, consider going for a leisurely stroll or a family hike to explore the park further.

Bike Paths: If your family enjoys biking, the park offers bike paths that connect to the larger regional trail system. You can bring your bicycles and go for a ride through the scenic landscape.

Pet-Friendly: Minnehaha Park is often pet-friendly, so you can bring your dogs along for a family outing. Be sure to follow park regulations regarding leashes and pet waste cleanup.

Accessibility: Efforts are made to ensure that the park is accessible to all visitors, including those with disabilities. This includes accessible pathways and facilities.

Visitor Services: The park may have visitor services, including information kiosks or visitor centers where you can obtain maps and brochures about the park's amenities.

Restrooms: Restroom facilities are typically available for park visitors.

Fishing: If your family enjoys fishing, you can bring your fishing gear and cast a line in the Mississippi River from designated fishing spots within the park.

Parking: Minnehaha Regional Park usually offers parking areas for visitors, but parking availability may vary depending on the season and time of day.

Trash and Recycling: Help keep the park clean by disposing of your trash and recyclables in designated bins.

Hours: The park's hours of operation may vary by season, so it's a good idea to check for current hours and any special events or activities.

Having a family picnic in Minnehaha Regional Park allows you to savor the natural beauty of Minnesota, share a meal together, and create cherished memories in a scenic and peaceful setting. It's an ideal location for spending quality time with loved ones in the great outdoors.

87. Explore the Sea Life Minnesota Aquarium.

Exploring the Sea Life Minnesota Aquarium at the Mall of America is a fascinating underwater adventure that offers visitors the chance to discover marine life from around the world. Here's what you can expect when you visit this captivating aquarium:

Marine Life Exhibits: Sea Life Minnesota Aquarium features a wide variety of marine life exhibits, showcasing everything from colorful tropical fish to majestic sea turtles and graceful sharks. You can observe and learn about creatures that inhabit oceans, seas, and freshwater environments.

Ocean Tunnel: One of the highlights of the aquarium is the Ocean Tunnel, a transparent walkway that allows you to stroll through a tunnel surrounded by 360-degree views of marine life. It's like walking on the ocean floor as sharks, rays, and other sea creatures swim above and around you.

Interactive Displays: Many exhibits include interactive displays and touch pools where you can get up close and personal with marine animals. You might have the opportunity to touch starfish, sea anemones, and other creatures under the guidance of knowledgeable staff.

Educational Presentations: Sea Life Minnesota often offers educational presentations and talks by marine experts. These presentations provide insights into the behaviors, adaptations, and conservation efforts related to marine life.

Conservation Initiatives: The aquarium is often involved in marine conservation efforts and may provide information about initiatives to protect and preserve ocean ecosystems and endangered species.

Children's Play Area: Some areas of the aquarium are designed with younger visitors in mind, featuring play zones, coloring stations, and interactive exhibits that are both fun and educational.

Accessibility: The aquarium typically strives to be accessible to all visitors, including those with disabilities, by providing accessible pathways and facilities.

Visitor Services: You'll usually find visitor services such as information desks and gift shops where you can obtain maps, brochures, and marine-themed merchandise.

Café and Dining Options: Depending on the facilities, there may be a café or dining options where you can enjoy a meal or snacks during or after your visit.

Hours and Tickets: The aquarium's hours of operation and ticket prices may vary by season and any special events. It's a good idea to check Sea Life Minnesota Aquarium's official website or contact them directly for current hours and admission fees.

Visiting the Sea Life Minnesota Aquarium is a chance to embark on an underwater journey, explore the mysteries of the deep, and gain a deeper appreciation for the incredible diversity of marine life that inhabits our oceans. Whether you're a marine enthusiast, a family with children, or simply looking for an engaging and educational experience, this aquarium offers a world of aquatic wonder to discover.

88.Attend a Minnesota Twins baseball game.

Attending a Minnesota Twins baseball game is a thrilling experience for baseball fans and sports enthusiasts. Here's what you can expect when you catch a game at Target Field, the Twins' home stadium:

Game-Day Atmosphere: The atmosphere at a Twins game is electric. Fans come together to support their team, and you'll feel the excitement in the air as you approach the stadium.

Target Field: Target Field is a state-of-the-art stadium known for its modern amenities and excellent fan experience. It offers comfortable seating, great sightlines, and a variety of food and beverage options.

Pre-Game Activities: Arrive early to enjoy pre-game activities. You can watch players warming up, explore the stadium, and soak in the energy of the crowd.

Concessions: Target Field has a wide range of concessions offering traditional ballpark favorites like hot dogs, popcorn, and peanuts, as well as specialty food items and local culinary treats.

Team Store: If you're a Twins fan, don't miss the team store. It's a great place to pick up Twins merchandise and souvenirs to remember your visit.

Family-Friendly: Twins games are family-friendly events. There are often family zones and activities for kids, making it a great outing for all ages.

Entertainment: Between innings, you can enjoy entertainment such as the Twins' mascot, T.C. Bear, and in-game contests. Big-screen displays also keep you updated on the action.

Fireworks Nights: Some games, especially during holidays or special occasions, feature post-game fireworks displays, adding to the excitement of the evening.

Theme Nights: The Twins often host theme nights, such as "Twin Cities Day" or "Military Appreciation Night," with special events and promotions.

Autographs: Depending on the game and circumstances, you might have the opportunity to get autographs from players, so bring a baseball or memorabilia if you're hoping for a signature.

Parking: Parking is typically available near the stadium, but it can get crowded on game days. Consider using public transportation or ride-sharing services if you prefer to avoid parking hassles.

Accessibility: Target Field is designed to be accessible to all visitors, including those with disabilities, with accessible seating, restrooms, and services.

Tickets: Ticket prices and availability can vary depending on the opponent and seating section. It's advisable to check the Minnesota Twins' official website or ticketing platforms for current ticket options and pricing.

Attending a Minnesota Twins baseball game is a quintessential American sports experience. It's a chance to enjoy America's pastime, cheer on your team, and immerse yourself in the excitement of a live baseball game. Whether you're a die-hard baseball fan or just looking for a fun outing with friends and family, a Twins game at Target Field is sure to be a memorable event.

89.Go horseback riding at Bunker Park Stable.

Horseback riding at Bunker Park Stable offers a scenic and enjoyable outdoor experience for riders of all skill levels. Here's what you can expect when you visit this equestrian facility:

Scenic Trails: Bunker Park Stable typically features scenic trails that wind through natural landscapes, including forests, fields, and open spaces. You'll have the opportunity to explore the beauty of the outdoors from a unique perspective on horseback.

Guided Trail Rides: The stable often offers guided trail rides led by experienced wranglers or guides. These knowledgeable staff members ensure the safety of riders and provide information about the natural surroundings during the ride.

Horses for All Levels: Bunker Park Stable usually has horses suitable for riders of all levels, from beginners to experienced equestrians. If you're new to horseback riding, the staff can help match you with a horse that suits your skill and comfort level.

Lessons and Training: In addition to trail rides, the stable may offer riding lessons and training sessions for individuals interested in improving their riding skills or learning the basics of horseback riding.

Group and Private Rides: You can often choose between group rides, where you ride with other visitors, or private rides for a more personalized experience. Group rides can be a fun way to socialize with fellow riders, while private rides offer solitude and individualized attention.

Safety Measures: Safety is a priority at equestrian facilities. You'll typically receive instructions on how to handle and interact with the horses safely, as well as wear appropriate riding gear, such as helmets.

Reservations: It's a good idea to make reservations in advance, especially during peak riding seasons, to ensure you have a spot for your desired ride.

Age Restrictions: There may be age restrictions for riders, with minimum age requirements for safety reasons. Be sure to check with Bunker Park Stable for their specific policies regarding age and weight limits.

Accessibility: Some equestrian facilities make efforts to accommodate riders with disabilities. If you or a member of your group has special needs, it's advisable to inquire about accessibility and accommodations.

Hours and Rates: The stable's hours of operation, rates, and policies may vary, so it's a good idea to check with Bunker Park Stable's official website or contact them directly for current information.

Horseback riding at Bunker Park Stable offers a chance to connect with nature, bond with these magnificent animals, and enjoy the serenity of the outdoors. Whether you're a seasoned rider or trying horseback riding for the first time, it's an opportunity to create lasting memories and experience the joy of equestrian adventure.

90. Take a paddlewheel riverboat tour on the Mississippi.

Taking a paddlewheel riverboat tour on the Mississippi River is a leisurely and scenic way to explore the waterways and learn about the history of the region. Here's what you can expect when you embark on such a tour:

Historic Paddlewheel Boats: Riverboat tours often feature historic paddlewheel boats, which are designed to replicate the grand vessels of the past. These boats have large, iconic paddlewheels on each side, which are not only functional but also add to the charm of the experience.

Narration and Guides: Most riverboat tours include narrated commentary by knowledgeable guides who provide insights into the history, culture, and landmarks along the river. You'll learn about the significance of the Mississippi River in American history.

Scenic Views: As you cruise along the river, you'll be treated to stunning views of the surrounding landscapes, including lush riverbanks, city skylines, and natural landmarks. It's an excellent opportunity for photography and enjoying the beauty of the outdoors.

Wildlife Viewing: Depending on the region and time of day, you may have the chance to spot local wildlife, including birds, fish, and occasionally, even bald eagles.

Themed Cruises: Some riverboat tours offer themed cruises, such as sunset cruises, brunch cruises, or holiday-themed excursions. These can provide unique and memorable experiences.

Dining Options: Depending on the tour, you may have the option to enjoy a meal or snacks on board. Riverboat dining can range from casual to fine dining experiences.

Entertainment: Some riverboat tours feature live entertainment, such as music or performances, to enhance the overall experience.

Accessibility: Efforts are usually made to ensure that riverboat tours are accessible to all passengers, including those with disabilities. This may include wheelchair ramps and accessible facilities.

Reservations: It's advisable to make reservations for riverboat tours, especially during peak tourist seasons, to secure your spot on the cruise of your choice.

Duration: Riverboat tours can vary in length, with options for short daytime cruises and longer, more comprehensive excursions. Be sure to check the duration of your chosen tour when making reservations.

Weather Considerations: Riverboat tours are typically offered seasonally, and weather conditions can impact scheduling. It's a good idea to check with the tour operator for availability and any weather-related updates.

Riverboat tours on the Mississippi River provide a unique perspective on the history and natural beauty of the region. Whether you're interested in learning about local culture, enjoying a relaxing cruise, or simply taking in the scenic views, a paddlewheel riverboat tour is a memorable way to experience the majesty of the Mississippi.

91.Attend the Minnesota State Fair in nearby St. Paul.

Attending the Minnesota State Fair in nearby St. Paul is a beloved annual tradition and a fun-filled event that offers a wide range of attractions and activities. Here's what you can expect when you visit this iconic fair:

Dates: The Minnesota State Fair typically takes place over 12 days in late August and early September. Be sure to check the official fair website for the exact dates and any updates.

Diverse Attractions: The fair features a diverse array of attractions, including carnival rides and games, live entertainment, agricultural exhibits, food vendors, arts and crafts displays, and much more.

Food Delights: The Minnesota State Fair is renowned for its eclectic and mouthwatering food offerings. You can sample a wide variety of fair foods, from classic corn dogs and cotton candy to unique creations like deep-fried candy bars, cheese curds, and gourmet dishes. Don't forget to try the famous "Pronto Pup" or "Sweet Martha's Cookies."

Live Entertainment: There are multiple stages and performance areas throughout the fairgrounds where you can enjoy live music, comedy shows, talent competitions, and other forms of entertainment. Check the fair's schedule for specific acts and performances.

Agricultural Exhibits: The fair celebrates Minnesota's agricultural heritage with livestock exhibits, agricultural demonstrations, and competitions showcasing animals, crops, and farm equipment.

Midway Rides: If you enjoy amusement rides, you'll find a bustling midway area with thrilling rides, games, and attractions. It's a great place for family fun and adrenaline-pumping adventures.

Creative Arts: The fair often features creative arts exhibits, where you can admire and purchase artwork, crafts, and handmade goods from local artisans.

Educational Exhibits: Learn about various topics, from science and technology to ecology and conservation, through interactive educational exhibits.

Kid-Friendly Activities: The fair is family-friendly, with dedicated areas for children's activities, games, and rides. The Mighty Midway and Kidway are popular spots for younger fairgoers.

Shopping: Explore rows of vendors selling clothing, accessories, home goods, and other products. It's an excellent place to shop for unique gifts and souvenirs.

Accessibility: Efforts are typically made to ensure the fairgrounds are accessible to all visitors, including those with disabilities.

Hours and Tickets: The fair's hours of operation, admission fees, and ticket options may vary by day and age group. Check the Minnesota State Fair's official website for the latest information on ticket prices and hours.

The Minnesota State Fair is a beloved tradition that attracts visitors from across the state and beyond. It's a celebration of culture, food, agriculture, and entertainment that offers something for everyone. Whether you're a foodie, a fan of live music, or simply looking for a day of family fun, the Minnesota State Fair is a must-visit event that captures the spirit of the region.

92.Experience the Minneapolis Aquatennial celebration.

Experiencing the Minneapolis Aquatennial celebration is a wonderful way to participate in the city's iconic summer festival, which typically features a wide range of activities and events. Here's what you can expect when you join in the Aquatennial festivities:

Dates: The Minneapolis Aquatennial celebration typically takes place in late July, spanning several days. Be sure to check the official Aquatennial website or local event calendars for the exact dates and schedule of events.

Fireworks: One of the highlights of the Aquatennial is the spectacular fireworks display that lights up the night sky over the Mississippi River. It's a dazzling show that draws crowds of spectators and is often accompanied by music.

Torchlight Parade: The Torchlight Parade is another major event during the Aquatennial. It features illuminated floats, marching bands, and local community groups that make their way through downtown Minneapolis. The parade is a beloved tradition and a great way to experience the city's vibrant spirit.

Beach Bash: The Aquatennial often includes a Beach Bash, which is a lakeside party featuring live music, games, food vendors, and activities for all ages. It's a fantastic way to relax by the water and enjoy the summer atmosphere.

Aquacades: The Aquatennial Aquacades typically include water-based activities and events along the shores of Lake Bde Maka Ska (formerly known as Lake Calhoun). These can include water skiing shows, sandcastle building contests, paddleboarding races, and more.

Milk Carton Boat Races: A quirky and entertaining tradition of the Aquatennial is the Milk Carton Boat Races. Participants create boats made entirely from milk cartons and then compete in races across a designated course on a local lake.

Outdoor Movies: Some Aquatennial events may include outdoor movie screenings, allowing you to enjoy a film under the stars in a park or other outdoor venue.

Music and Entertainment: Throughout the celebration, you can expect live music performances, entertainment acts, and cultural showcases featuring local and regional talent.

Food and Beverage: Food trucks and vendors often line the streets and festival grounds, offering a variety of culinary delights, from classic fair foods to international cuisines.

Family-Friendly: Many Aquatennial events are family-friendly, with activities and entertainment suitable for all ages.

Accessibility: Efforts are usually made to ensure that Aquatennial events and venues are accessible to all visitors, including those with disabilities.

Parade Route and Schedule: Be sure to check the official Aquatennial website for the parade route, schedule of events, and any updates related to specific activities or performances.

The Minneapolis Aquatennial celebration is a time-honored tradition that brings the community together to celebrate summer, culture, and the vibrant spirit of the city. Whether you're interested in watching fireworks, enjoying live music, or participating in quirky events like the Milk Carton Boat Races, the Aquatennial offers a wide range of experiences that capture the essence of Minneapolis during the summer months.

93.Enjoy the Minneapolis St. Paul International Film Festival.

The Minneapolis St. Paul International Film Festival (MSPIFF) is an exciting cultural event that showcases a diverse array of films from around the world. Here's what you can expect when you attend this prestigious film festival:

Dates: MSPIFF typically takes place over several weeks in the spring, usually in April. Be sure to check the official festival website for the exact dates and schedule.

Film Screenings: The heart of MSPIFF is its extensive lineup of film screenings. The festival typically features a wide variety of films, including narrative features, documentaries, short films, and international cinema. These films often explore diverse themes, cultures, and genres, making it a great opportunity to discover new voices and perspectives in cinema.

World Cinema: MSPIFF often spotlights world cinema, offering audiences the chance to explore films from different countries and cultures. It's a window into global storytelling and filmmaking.

Independent Films: Independent filmmakers often showcase their work at MSPIFF, making it a hub for emerging talent and innovative storytelling. You may have the opportunity to watch films that challenge conventions and push the boundaries of cinema.

Special Presentations: The festival may include special presentations, screenings of classic films, director Q&A sessions, and panel discussions that provide insights into the filmmaking process and industry trends.

Awards and Recognition: MSPIFF often includes awards ceremonies to recognize outstanding films and filmmakers. Attendees can watch award-winning films and celebrate cinematic achievements.

Cultural Diversity: The festival celebrates cultural diversity and often includes films that explore themes of identity, social justice, and human rights. It's a platform for thought-provoking and impactful storytelling.

Venues: Film screenings typically take place in various venues across Minneapolis and St. Paul, including independent theaters, cultural centers, and festival-specific venues. Be sure to check the festival program for venue details.

Tickets and Passes: MSPIFF offers various ticketing options, including single tickets for individual screenings and festival passes for access to multiple films. Early ticket purchases are advisable for popular screenings.

Accessibility: Efforts are usually made to ensure that festival venues are accessible to all attendees, including those with disabilities.

Networking: MSPIFF often attracts filmmakers, industry professionals, and cinephiles. It provides opportunities for networking, connecting with fellow film enthusiasts, and engaging in discussions about cinema.

Local and International Talent: You may have the chance to interact with filmmakers, actors, and industry insiders during screenings and special events.

Food and Refreshments: Some festival venues may offer food and refreshments, allowing you to enjoy a meal or snack before or after screenings.

The Minneapolis St. Paul International Film Festival is a cultural gem that brings the magic of cinema to the Twin Cities. Whether you're a film aficionado, a casual moviegoer, or simply curious about global cinema, MSPIFF offers a dynamic and enriching cinematic experience. It's a platform for storytelling, cultural exchange, and the celebration of the art of filmmaking. Be sure to check the festival's official website for the latest updates, program details, and ticketing information as you plan your visit.

94. Attend the Minneapolis Pride Festival.

Attending the Minneapolis Pride Festival is a vibrant and inclusive celebration of LGBTQ+ culture and community. Here's what you can expect when you join in the festivities:

Travel to Minneapolis Minnesota

Dates: The Minneapolis Pride Festival typically takes place in late June and is part of Pride Month, which is celebrated nationwide. Be sure to check the official festival website for the exact dates and schedule of events.

Pride Parade: The festival often kicks off with a colorful and lively Pride Parade that winds through the streets of Minneapolis. The parade features a diverse array of floats, marching bands, community organizations, and LGBTQ+ allies. It's a joyful and spirited procession that celebrates the diversity of the LGBTQ+ community.

Festival Grounds: The heart of the celebration is the festival grounds, which are usually set up in a central location, such as Loring Park. The festival grounds feature a variety of activities and attractions:

Entertainment: Enjoy live performances by local and national LGBTQ+ artists and entertainers on multiple stages. The music and entertainment lineup often includes musicians, drag queens, dancers, and comedians.

Vendor Booths: Explore vendor booths and exhibits by LGBTQ+ organizations, community groups, businesses, and artists. You can shop for pride merchandise, art, clothing, and more.

Food and Drink: Savor a wide range of culinary delights from food trucks and vendors. You'll find diverse options to satisfy your taste buds.

Community Resources: Connect with LGBTQ+ community organizations and resources that provide support, education, and advocacy.

Family Zone: Many Pride Festivals have family-friendly areas with activities for children, making it an inclusive event for families of all backgrounds.

Cultural Celebrations: The festival celebrates LGBTQ+ culture, history, and achievements. It's an opportunity to learn about the contributions of the LGBTQ+ community to art, music, literature, and social progress.

Diversity and Inclusivity: The Minneapolis Pride Festival emphasizes diversity and inclusivity, welcoming people of all sexual orientations, gender identities, and backgrounds. It's a safe and affirming space for everyone.

Equality and Advocacy: Pride Festivals often serve as platforms for advocacy and raising awareness of LGBTQ+ rights and issues. You may have the chance to engage with organizations that promote equality and social justice.

Accessibility: Efforts are usually made to ensure that festival venues are accessible to all attendees, including those with disabilities.

Parade Grand Marshals: The Pride Parade often features grand marshals who are recognized for their contributions to the LGBTQ+ community and social justice causes.

Community Engagement: The festival provides opportunities to connect with LGBTQ+ community members, allies, and advocates. It's a chance to celebrate love, acceptance, and unity.

Health and Wellness: Some Pride Festivals include health and wellness resources, such as free HIV testing and information about LGBTQ+-friendly healthcare providers.

Volunteer Opportunities: If you're interested in getting involved, many Pride Festivals offer volunteer opportunities to support the event and contribute to its success.

The Minneapolis Pride Festival is a joyful and inclusive celebration of LGBTQ+ pride, culture, and progress. It's a time to come together, celebrate diversity, and show support for LGBTQ+ rights and equality. Whether you're a member of the LGBTQ+ community or an ally, attending the festival is a wonderful way to participate in a vibrant and accepting community event. Be sure to check the official festival website for the latest updates and details as you plan your visit.

95.Celebrate the Holidazzle Festival during the holiday season.

Celebrating the Holidazzle Festival during the holiday season is a festive and magical experience that brings the spirit of the holidays to downtown Minneapolis. Here's what you can expect when you join in the festivities:

Dates: The Holidazzle Festival typically takes place during the holiday season, running from late November through December. Be sure to check the official festival website for the exact dates and schedule of events.

Downtown Minneapolis: The festival is centered in downtown Minneapolis, often taking place in Loring Park or another prominent downtown location. The area is transformed into a winter wonderland with holiday decorations, lights, and a festive atmosphere.

Holiday Lights: One of the highlights of Holidazzle is the dazzling holiday light displays. You can expect to see beautifully lit trees, sparkling decorations, and illuminated sculptures that create a magical ambiance after dark.

Ice Skating: Some Holidazzle festivals include an outdoor ice skating rink where you can lace up your skates and glide across the ice. Skating under the twinkling lights adds to the holiday charm.

Vendor Village: Explore a Vendor Village featuring local artisans and craft vendors. It's a great place to shop for unique holiday gifts, ornaments, and seasonal treats.

Food and Beverages: Sample a variety of festive foods and beverages, including hot cocoa, mulled wine, holiday-themed dishes, and sweet treats. Food trucks and vendors often offer a range of options to satisfy your cravings.

Entertainment: Enjoy live entertainment, including holiday music, performances, and even visits from Santa Claus himself. Check the festival schedule for specific performances and activities.

Holiday Shopping: Downtown Minneapolis is home to many shops and boutiques, making it a great place to do some holiday shopping. You can explore local stores and find special gifts for your loved ones.

Children's Activities: Holidazzle often includes family-friendly activities and attractions for children, such as holiday crafts, storytelling, and visits with Santa.

Parade: In some years, Holidazzle may feature a holiday parade with illuminated floats, marching bands, and costumed characters. The parade is a highlight for families and parade enthusiasts.

Accessibility: Efforts are typically made to ensure that festival venues and activities are accessible to all attendees, including those with disabilities.

Festival of Lights: Some Holidazzle festivals conclude with a spectacular Festival of Lights parade and fireworks display, marking the culmination of the holiday festivities.

Fireworks: Fireworks are a common feature of Holidazzle, adding to the festive atmosphere. The vibrant colors lighting up the night sky are a perfect way to celebrate the season.

Admission: Holidazzle festivals are often free to attend, with opportunities to purchase food, beverages, and merchandise.

The Holidazzle Festival is a beloved Minneapolis tradition that brings the community together to celebrate the holiday season. Whether you're looking to enjoy the holiday lights, indulge in seasonal treats, shop for gifts, or simply soak in the festive atmosphere, Holidazzle offers a joyful and heartwarming experience. Be sure to check the official festival website for the latest updates and details as you plan your visit during the holiday season.

96. Visit the Uptown Art Fair.

Visiting the Uptown Art Fair is a delightful way to experience a vibrant showcase of art, culture, and creativity in Minneapolis. Here's what you can expect when you attend this popular art fair:

Dates: The Uptown Art Fair typically takes place in early August. Be sure to check the official art fair website for the exact dates and schedule of events.

Location: The fair is located in the Uptown neighborhood of Minneapolis, known for its trendy atmosphere and artistic community. The fair usually spans several blocks of Hennepin Avenue and its surrounding streets.

Art Exhibits: The heart of the Uptown Art Fair is, of course, the art itself. You'll have the opportunity to explore a diverse array of artwork created by talented artists from around the country. The art on display often includes paintings, sculptures, photography, ceramics, jewelry, textiles, and more.

Artist Booths: Artists typically set up booths to showcase and sell their creations. It's a fantastic opportunity to meet the artists, discuss their work, and perhaps even purchase a unique piece of art to take home.

Juried Show: The Uptown Art Fair is known for its juried art show, which means that a panel of experts selects the participating artists and their works. This ensures a high level of quality and diversity in the art on display.

Live Entertainment: The fair often features live music and entertainment, adding to the festive atmosphere. Musicians, bands, and performers take to the stages to provide a soundtrack to your art exploration.

Food and Beverages: You can enjoy a variety of culinary delights from food trucks and vendors stationed throughout the fair. Whether you're craving savory or sweet treats, you'll find options to satisfy your taste buds.

Beer and Wine Garden: Some Uptown Art Fairs include a beer and wine garden where you can relax, sip on local brews or wine, and take in the sights and sounds of the fair.

Family-Friendly Activities: The art fair is family-friendly and often includes activities for children, such as art workshops, face painting, and interactive art displays.

Shopping: Beyond art, the fair may host boutique vendors selling clothing, accessories, home goods, and other unique items.

Accessibility: Efforts are usually made to ensure that the fair is accessible to all attendees, including those with disabilities.

Parking and Transportation: Plan ahead for parking or consider using public transportation to get to the fair, as Uptown can be busy during the event.

Free Admission: The Uptown Art Fair is typically free to attend, although you may want to bring cash or cards for art purchases and food.

The Uptown Art Fair is a celebration of creativity and a chance to immerse yourself in the world of art. Whether you're a seasoned art enthusiast or simply appreciate the beauty of artistic expression, the fair offers a wonderful opportunity to engage with the local and national art scene, discover new talents, and perhaps find that perfect piece of art to adorn your home. Be sure to check the official art fair website for the latest updates and details as you plan your visit in August.

97.Attend the Stone Arch Bridge Festival.

Attending the Stone Arch Bridge Festival is a fantastic way to celebrate art, music, and community in the heart of Minneapolis. Here's what you can expect when you participate in this vibrant festival:

Dates: The Stone Arch Bridge Festival typically takes place in mid-June. Be sure to check the official festival website for the exact dates and schedule of events.

Location: The festival is held in the historic Mill District of Minneapolis, with the picturesque Stone Arch Bridge as its backdrop. The Mill District is known for its rich history, cultural significance, and scenic riverfront views.

Art Exhibits: The festival is primarily an art-focused event, featuring a wide range of artistic creations. You can explore and purchase original works of art, including paintings, sculptures, photography, jewelry, ceramics, textiles, and more.

Artist Booths: Talented artists from Minnesota and beyond set up booths to showcase their work and interact with visitors. This is an excellent opportunity to meet the artists, learn about their creative process, and acquire unique pieces of art.

Juried Art Show: The festival often includes a juried art show, ensuring that the participating artists and their works meet a high standard of quality. It's a curated selection of art that represents a diverse range of styles and media.

Live Music: The festival features live music performances by local and regional musicians and bands. You can enjoy a variety of musical genres, from folk and blues to rock and jazz, while taking in the scenic surroundings.

Food and Beverages: Savor a wide array of culinary delights from food vendors and trucks. Whether you're in the mood for savory or sweet treats, you'll find an assortment of options to satisfy your taste buds.

Beer and Wine Garden: Some Stone Arch Bridge Festivals include a beer and wine garden where you can relax with a beverage and enjoy the live music and art.

Family-Friendly Activities: The festival offers family-friendly activities, including art activities for children, face painting, and interactive art displays.

Mississippi River Views: The location of the festival along the Mississippi River provides a stunning backdrop for art appreciation and leisurely strolls along the riverbanks.

Shopping: Beyond art, you can shop for unique clothing, accessories, home goods, and more from boutique vendors.

Accessibility: Efforts are usually made to ensure that the festival is accessible to all attendees, including those with disabilities.

Free Admission: The Stone Arch Bridge Festival is typically free to attend, though you may want to bring cash or cards for art purchases and food.

The Stone Arch Bridge Festival is a celebration of creativity, community, and culture in one of Minneapolis' most scenic locations. Whether you're a seasoned art enthusiast, a music lover, or simply looking for a relaxing day by the river, the festival offers a welcoming and vibrant atmosphere to explore, appreciate, and support the arts. Be sure to check the official festival website for the latest updates and details as you plan your visit in June.

98.Experience the Minneapolis Fringe Festival.

Experiencing the Minneapolis Fringe Festival is an exciting way to immerse yourself in the world of performing arts and independent theater. Here's what you can expect when you attend this dynamic and creative festival:

Dates: The Minneapolis Fringe Festival typically takes place over a span of about 10 days in early to mid-August. Be sure to check the official festival website for the exact dates and schedule of performances.

Venues: The festival utilizes a variety of venues across Minneapolis, including theaters, galleries, and unconventional spaces. Each venue hosts multiple performances throughout the festival.

Diverse Performances: The Fringe Festival showcases a wide range of performances, including plays, musicals, dance, comedy, experimental theater, and more. You can expect a diverse lineup of shows that push boundaries and challenge conventions.

Local and National Talent: The festival features both local talent and artists from around the country. It's a platform for emerging playwrights, actors, directors, and theater companies to showcase their work.

Original Works: Many of the productions at the Fringe Festival are original works that may be making their debut. It's an opportunity to see cutting-edge and thought-provoking theater.

Accessibility: Efforts are typically made to ensure that festival venues are accessible to all attendees, including those with disabilities.

Fringe Central: Look for the "Fringe Central" hub, where you can gather with other festivalgoers, purchase tickets, and get information about the festival. It's often a hub of activity and a great place to meet fellow theater enthusiasts.

Ticketing: The festival operates on a ticketing system where you purchase individual tickets for the shows you want to see. Some festivals offer multi-show passes for added convenience.

Community Atmosphere: The Fringe Festival creates a sense of community among artists and audiences alike. It's a time when theater lovers come together to celebrate the performing arts and engage in lively discussions about the shows they've seen.

Late-Night Shows: The festival often includes late-night performances, which can be edgier and more experimental in nature. These shows are a unique and exciting aspect of the Fringe experience.

Fringe Awards: At the end of the festival, awards may be given to outstanding productions and performers. It's a chance to celebrate and recognize artistic excellence.

Affordability: The Minneapolis Fringe Festival is known for its affordability, making it accessible to a wide range of audiences. Tickets are typically reasonably priced, and there are often special deals and discounts available.

Outdoor Performances: In addition to indoor venues, some festivals may feature outdoor performances, street theater, and interactive experiences in public spaces.

The Minneapolis Fringe Festival is a celebration of creativity, innovation, and the performing arts. It's a chance to discover new voices in theater, explore diverse narratives, and engage with thought-provoking performances. Whether you're a seasoned theatergoer or new to the world of fringe theater, the festival offers a welcoming and immersive experience. Be sure to check the official festival website for the latest updates, show listings, and ticket information as you plan your visit in August.

99.Participate in the Twin Cities Marathon.

Participating in the Twin Cities Marathon is an incredible and rewarding athletic endeavor that takes you on a scenic journey through the beautiful cities of Minneapolis and St. Paul. Here's what you can expect when you decide to take on this iconic marathon:

Date: The Twin Cities Marathon typically takes place on the first Sunday in October. Be sure to check the official marathon website for the exact date and any updates related to the event.

Race Start: The marathon begins in downtown Minneapolis near U.S. Bank Stadium and finishes near the State Capitol in St. Paul. The point-to-point course provides an opportunity to see many of the Twin Cities' landmarks.

Scenic Course: The marathon course is known for its scenic beauty and showcases the picturesque landscapes of the Minneapolis and St. Paul metropolitan area. You'll run along lakes, rivers, tree-lined streets, and through charming neighborhoods.

Runner Support: The event provides ample runner support, including aid stations with water, sports drinks, and medical assistance. There are also designated cheering sections along the route to motivate and encourage runners.

Entertainment: You'll enjoy live music and entertainment at various points along the course, adding to the festive atmosphere.

Marathon Expo: Before the race, there's typically a marathon expo where participants can pick up their race packets, browse running-related merchandise, and connect with other runners.

Finish Line Festival: The finish line is a celebratory atmosphere with a festival-like vibe. Friends, family, and spectators gather to welcome and support the runners as they cross the finish line.

Medals and Awards: Finishers receive a commemorative medal to celebrate their achievement. The event may also include awards for top finishers in various categories.

Charity Partners: The Twin Cities Marathon often partners with local charities, allowing runners to raise funds for important causes while participating in the race.

Accessibility: Efforts are made to ensure that the marathon is accessible to runners of all abilities. Wheelchair divisions and adaptive sports categories may be available.

Registration: Registration for the Twin Cities Marathon typically opens several months before the event. It's advisable to register early, as spots can fill up quickly.

Training: Preparing for a marathon requires consistent training and dedication. Many runners follow training plans that gradually build up their mileage to prepare for the 26.2-mile distance.

Spectators: The marathon is not only a rewarding experience for runners but also for spectators who come out to support their friends and loved ones. Spectators often line the streets, offering cheers, signs, and encouragement.

Post-Race Celebration: After completing the marathon, many runners celebrate their achievement by dining at local restaurants, enjoying a well-deserved meal, and sharing their experiences with fellow runners and supporters.

The Twin Cities Marathon is not just a race; it's an unforgettable journey through two vibrant cities with a supportive and enthusiastic running community. Whether you're an experienced marathoner or taking on the challenge for the first time, participating in this marathon is a testament to your dedication and endurance. Be sure to visit the official marathon website for detailed information, registration, and any updates regarding the event.

100.Attend the MayDay Parade and Festival.

Attending the MayDay Parade and Festival is a unique and vibrant experience that celebrates community, art, and the arrival of spring. Here's what you can expect when you join in the festivities:

Date: The MayDay Parade and Festival typically takes place on the first Sunday in May. Be sure to check the official event website for the exact date and schedule of events.

Travel to Minneapolis Minnesota

Location: The event is held in the Powderhorn Park neighborhood of Minneapolis, with the parade route and festival grounds centered around Powderhorn Park itself.

MayDay Parade: The heart of the event is the MayDay Parade, a colorful and imaginative procession featuring giant puppets, stilt walkers, community members, and local artists. The parade often follows a theme related to the environment, social justice, or community unity.

Parade Route: The parade winds its way through the streets of the Powderhorn Park neighborhood, offering a unique and dynamic viewing experience. Spectators gather along the route to watch the creative and whimsical parade entries.

Giant Puppets: The MayDay Parade is known for its impressive giant puppets, which are crafted by local artists and community members. These puppets often represent themes related to nature, sustainability, and social change.

Music and Performances: The parade features live music, drumming, dancing, and other performances that add to the festive atmosphere. Local musicians and artists participate in the event, creating a lively and dynamic celebration.

Festival in the Park: After the parade, the festivities continue with a festival in Powderhorn Park. The park comes alive with art installations, craft vendors, food trucks, and community organizations. It's a great opportunity to explore local art and crafts, sample diverse cuisines, and connect with community groups.

Community Engagement: The MayDay Parade and Festival emphasize community engagement and social justice. Many participating organizations use the event as a platform to raise awareness about important issues and promote positive change.

Family-Friendly Activities: The event is family-friendly and often includes activities for children, such as art workshops, face painting, and interactive art installations.

Sustainability: Efforts are made to ensure that the event is environmentally conscious. You may find recycling stations, composting options, and educational resources related to sustainability.

Art and Craft Fair: The festival includes an art and craft fair where local artisans and vendors display and sell their creations. It's an opportunity to support local artists and find unique handmade items.

Accessibility: The organizers typically make efforts to ensure that the festival is accessible to all attendees, including those with disabilities.

Free Admission: The MayDay Parade and Festival are typically free to attend, although you may want to bring cash for purchases from vendors and food trucks.

The MayDay Parade and Festival in Powderhorn Park is a one-of-a-kind event that celebrates creativity, community, and the arrival of spring. Whether you're an art enthusiast, a supporter of social causes, or simply looking for a joyful and inclusive celebration, this event offers a memorable and inspiring experience. Be sure to check the official event website for the latest updates, theme details, and schedule as you plan your visit in May.

101.Take a hot air balloon ride over the city.

Taking a hot air balloon ride over Minneapolis is a breathtaking and memorable experience that provides a unique perspective of the city's skyline and scenic landscapes. Here's what you can expect when you embark on a hot air balloon adventure:

Booking: Start by booking your hot air balloon ride with a reputable and licensed balloon operator. They will provide you with details about the date, time, meeting location, and any specific instructions.

Launch Site: On the day of your ride, you'll typically meet at a designated launch site, often located in a picturesque area outside the city. This is where the balloon will be inflated and prepared for flight.

Pre-flight Briefing: Your experienced balloon pilot will provide you with a pre-flight briefing, explaining safety procedures, what to expect during the ride, and answering any questions you may have.

Balloon Inflation: Witness the fascinating process of inflating the hot air balloon. As the balloon takes shape and rises, you'll have the opportunity to assist the crew or simply observe.

Takeoff: Once the balloon is inflated and the pilot gives the green light, it's time to climb into the basket. As the hot air balloon gently lifts off the ground, you'll experience the exhilarating sensation of ascending into the sky.

Scenic Views: As you ascend higher, you'll be treated to breathtaking panoramic views of Minneapolis and its surroundings. You'll see the city's skyline, parks, lakes, and landmarks from a completely different perspective.

Peaceful Flight: Hot air balloon rides are known for their tranquility. You'll enjoy a serene and peaceful journey, with only the sound of the wind and occasional bursts of the burner flame.

Floating Experience: Unlike other forms of flight, hot air ballooning offers a sensation of floating. The balloon moves with the wind, providing a gentle and smooth ride.

Photography: Don't forget to bring your camera or smartphone to capture the incredible vistas from above. The unique angles and perspectives make for stunning photographs.

Duration: Hot air balloon rides typically last about an hour, although the total experience, including preparation and post-flight celebrations, may take several hours.

Landing: Your pilot will carefully guide the balloon to a suitable landing spot. Once on the ground, you can assist with deflating the balloon or simply enjoy the post-flight celebration.

Champagne Toast: Many hot air balloon rides conclude with a traditional champagne toast to celebrate the adventure. It's a memorable way to cap off your experience.

Certificate: Some balloon operators provide a flight certificate or a souvenir to commemorate your hot air balloon ride.

Dress Comfortably: Dress in layers and wear comfortable clothing appropriate for the weather. It can be cooler at higher altitudes, so be prepared.

Weather-Dependent: Hot air balloon rides are weather-dependent, and flights may be rescheduled if conditions are not suitable for safe flying.

Shared Experience: Hot air balloon rides are often shared experiences, with multiple passengers in the basket. It's a great opportunity to share the adventure with friends or family.

A hot air balloon ride over Minneapolis offers a serene and awe-inspiring way to see the city and its surroundings. It's a unique and unforgettable experience that provides a fresh perspective on familiar landscapes. As you float peacefully above the city, you'll create lasting memories and capture stunning views from the sky. Be sure to book your ride with a reputable operator and prepare for an adventure you'll cherish for a lifetime.

102. Explore the Minneapolis Skyway System.

Exploring the Minneapolis Skyway System is a unique and convenient way to navigate the city while staying protected from the elements, especially during the cold winter months. Here's what you can expect when you venture into this extensive network of indoor walkways:

What is the Skyway System?
The Minneapolis Skyway System is a vast network of enclosed pedestrian walkways that connect various buildings, offices, hotels, restaurants, and other establishments in downtown Minneapolis. It spans several miles and is designed to provide year-round climate-controlled access throughout the city center.

Accessibility: The Skyway System is accessible to the public and free to use. You can enter and exit the skyways at numerous points throughout downtown Minneapolis. Look for signs or maps to help you navigate.

Climate Control: One of the primary advantages of the Skyway System is climate control. Whether it's scorching hot in the summer or bitterly cold in the winter, you can comfortably traverse the city without exposure to extreme weather conditions.

Maps and Signage: To make navigation easier, you'll find maps and directional signage posted at key junctions within the skyways. These maps can help you find your way to specific destinations.

Travel to Minneapolis Minnesota

Connecting Buildings: The Skyway System connects numerous buildings, including office towers, shopping centers, hotels, government buildings, and more. You can easily access a range of services, including restaurants, shops, and services, without having to go outside.

Diverse Dining Options: Many restaurants and eateries are located within the Skyway System. It's a great place to explore a variety of dining options, from quick bites to fine dining, all while staying comfortably indoors.

Shopping: The Skyway System is home to numerous shops and boutiques. Whether you're looking for clothing, gifts, or specialty items, you'll find a wide array of shopping opportunities.

Skyway Art: Keep an eye out for art installations and displays that are often featured in the skyways. Minneapolis has a thriving arts scene, and the skyways provide a unique gallery space.

Business District: The Skyway System is integrated with Minneapolis' central business district, making it a practical choice for professionals working in the area.

Hours of Operation: It's important to note that the Skyway System is generally open during regular business hours. Some sections may close in the evenings and on weekends, so it's a good idea to check the hours of specific segments if you plan to explore outside typical business hours.

Security and Safety: The Skyway System is typically safe, well-lit, and monitored by security personnel. However, it's advisable to take standard precautions and be aware of your surroundings when using any public space.

Parking: If you're driving into downtown Minneapolis, you can often find parking ramps or lots that provide convenient access to the Skyway System. Be sure to check parking options in advance.

Exploring the Minneapolis Skyway System is not only a practical way to get around but also an opportunity to experience the city's vibrant downtown scene while staying comfortably indoors. Whether you're a local resident or a visitor, the Skyway System offers a unique and convenient way to discover all that downtown Minneapolis has to offer.

103.Go indoor skydiving at iFLY Minneapolis.

Indoor skydiving at iFLY Minneapolis offers an exhilarating and safe way to experience the sensation of freefalling without jumping out of an airplane. Here's what you can expect when you take part in this thrilling adventure:

iFLY Experience: iFLY is an indoor skydiving facility that uses vertical wind tunnels to create a controlled and realistic skydiving experience. It's suitable for individuals of various ages and skill levels, from beginners to experienced skydivers.

Pre-Flight Preparation: Before your flight, you'll receive a pre-flight briefing from a certified instructor. This briefing covers safety procedures, body positions, hand signals, and what to expect during your flight.

Gear and Equipment: iFLY provides all the necessary gear and equipment, including a flight suit, helmet, goggles, and earplugs. You'll also wear specialized indoor skydiving shoes.

Flight Chamber: The heart of the experience is the vertical wind tunnel, a chamber with a powerful updraft of air. You'll enter the chamber with your instructor and experience the sensation of floating on a cushion of air.

Instructor-Guided Flight: During your flight, a certified instructor will accompany you in the chamber to ensure your safety and guide you through the experience. They'll assist with body positioning and help you make the most of your flight.

Controlled Freefall: The wind tunnel generates enough lift to simulate the sensation of freefalling during a skydive. You'll have the opportunity to control your body's position and movements, including turns and spins.

Duration: A typical iFLY flight experience includes two one-minute sessions in the wind tunnel, which is equivalent to two freefall skydives from a plane.

Spectator-Friendly: iFLY facilities often have observation areas where friends and family can watch your flight and take photographs or videos.

Post-Flight Debrief: After your flight, you'll have a post-flight debriefing with your instructor to discuss your experience and receive feedback.

Additional Packages: iFLY offers various packages, including options for additional flight time and personalized experiences. You can also purchase photos and videos of your flight.

Reservations: It's advisable to make a reservation in advance to secure your flight time, especially during peak hours or busy seasons.

Safety: iFLY takes safety seriously, and instructors are highly trained to ensure a safe and enjoyable experience for all participants.

Accessibility: iFLY facilities are typically accessible to individuals with disabilities, and accommodations can be made to accommodate various needs.

Indoor skydiving at iFLY Minneapolis provides an adrenaline-pumping adventure in a controlled environment. It's a thrilling activity suitable for solo adventurers, groups, families, and even team-building outings. Whether you're a first-time flyer or a seasoned skydiver looking for a unique experience, iFLY offers a safe and unforgettable way to experience the sensation of flight and freefall. Be sure to check with iFLY Minneapolis for specific details, pricing, and reservations as you plan your indoor skydiving adventure.

104.Take a brewery tour at a local craft brewery.

Taking a brewery tour at a local craft brewery in Minneapolis offers a behind-the-scenes look at the brewing process and a chance to sample some delicious and unique beers. Here's what you can expect when you embark on a brewery tour:

Selecting a Brewery: Minneapolis has a thriving craft beer scene with several local breweries to choose from. Research and choose a brewery that interests you or is known for its particular style of beer.

Reservations: Some breweries require reservations for their tours, especially if you're visiting with a group. It's a good idea to check the brewery's website or call ahead to inquire about availability and any reservation requirements.

Tour Duration: Brewery tours typically last around 30 minutes to an hour, although this can vary by brewery. Some breweries offer longer and more in-depth tours, while others focus more on the tasting experience.

Guided Tour: A knowledgeable brewery guide will lead you through the brewing facilities, explaining the beer-making process, the ingredients used, and the equipment involved. You'll get to see the brewing tanks, fermentation vessels, and more.

Beer Sampling: One of the highlights of a brewery tour is the beer tasting. You'll have the opportunity to sample a selection of the brewery's beers. Some tours include a flight of beers, while others may offer specific tastings.

Tasting Room: Many breweries have tasting rooms or taprooms where you can enjoy additional beers after the tour. This is a great opportunity to try more of their offerings and relax with friends or fellow tour participants.

Q&A: During the tour and tasting, you're encouraged to ask questions about the brewing process, the brewery's history, and the specific beers you're trying. Brewers and guides are usually happy to share their knowledge.

Souvenirs: Some brewery tours include souvenirs, such as a branded glass, pint glass, or other merchandise. Check in advance to see if any extras are included with your tour.

Closed-Toe Shoes: Some breweries may require guests to wear closed-toe shoes for safety reasons. It's a good idea to check the brewery's dress code policy in advance.

Designated Driver: If you're part of a group, consider having a designated driver who refrains from drinking during the tour to ensure everyone's safety.

Responsible Drinking: Enjoy the beer tasting responsibly, and know your limits. Many breweries offer water to help cleanse your palate between tastings.

Local Food: Some breweries partner with local food trucks or have on-site restaurants where you can enjoy a meal to complement your beer.

Variety of Breweries: Minneapolis offers a wide variety of craft breweries, from small neighborhood brewpubs to larger production facilities. Explore different breweries to discover various beer styles and atmospheres.

Brewery tours are not only educational but also a fun way to appreciate the craftsmanship and artistry that goes into making craft beer. Whether you're a beer enthusiast or simply looking for a unique and enjoyable experience, a brewery tour in Minneapolis is a great way to spend an afternoon or evening. Be sure to check with the specific brewery for tour details, pricing, and availability as you plan your visit.

105.Try your hand at ax throwing at a local venue.

Trying your hand at axe throwing at a local venue in Minneapolis is a fun and unique activity that provides a mix of skill, competition, and enjoyment. Here's what you can expect when you give axe throwing a try:

Venue Selection: Minneapolis has several axe throwing venues that offer a safe and controlled environment for this activity. Research and choose a venue that suits your preferences, whether it's a lively and social atmosphere or a more laid-back experience.

Safety Briefing: When you arrive at the axe throwing venue, you'll typically receive a safety briefing from experienced instructors. They will explain the rules, safety guidelines, and proper throwing techniques.

Axe Selection: Venues provide a variety of axes for different skill levels, and instructors will help you select an axe that suits your ability and comfort level.

Throwing Techniques: Instructors will teach you the proper techniques for throwing an axe, including how to grip, stance, and release. You'll have the opportunity to practice your throws before engaging in any games or competitions.

Games and Challenges: Axe throwing venues often offer a range of games and challenges to make the experience competitive and entertaining. Popular games include hitting specific targets or aiming for the coveted bullseye.

Friendly Competition: Axe throwing is a social activity that's perfect for group outings with friends, family, or colleagues. You can engage in friendly competitions and keep score to see who can hit the most targets.

Instructor Guidance: Instructors are available throughout your session to provide tips, guidance, and encouragement. They can help you improve your throwing skills and offer advice on achieving better accuracy.

Safety Measures: Safety is a top priority at axe throwing venues. You'll be provided with safety gear, including safety goggles and wristbands. Follow all safety rules and listen to your instructors for a safe and enjoyable experience.

Food and Drinks: Some venues have on-site bars or allow you to bring your own food and drinks. It's a good idea to check the venue's policy on refreshments.

Private Events: Many axe throwing venues offer private event bookings, making it a great choice for birthday parties, bachelor/bachelorette parties, team-building events, and corporate outings.

Age Restrictions: Age restrictions may apply, so check with the venue regarding the minimum age for participants.

Reservations: Axe throwing has gained popularity, so it's advisable to make reservations in advance, especially if you're visiting with a group or during peak hours.

Accessible Fun: Axe throwing can be enjoyed by people of various skill levels and physical abilities. It's a great way to try something new and have a blast while doing it.

Axe throwing is not only a thrilling and unique experience but also an opportunity to challenge yourself and have a great time with friends and family. Whether you're celebrating a special occasion or simply looking for a memorable adventure, axe throwing at a local venue in Minneapolis provides an entertaining and skill-building activity. Be sure to check with the specific venue for details, pricing, and reservation information as you plan your axe throwing outing.

106. Visit the Minnesota Transportation Museum.

Visiting the Minnesota Transportation Museum offers a fascinating journey through the state's transportation history. Here's what you can expect when you explore this captivating museum:

Location: The Minnesota Transportation Museum is located in St. Paul, Minnesota, at the Jackson Street Roundhouse, which is a historic railroad maintenance facility.

Historical Significance: The Jackson Street Roundhouse itself is historically significant as it was once a working railroad roundhouse where steam locomotives were serviced and turned around for their next journeys. The museum's location adds an authentic touch to the experience.

Railroad Exhibits: The museum features a wide range of railroad-related exhibits, artifacts, and memorabilia. You'll have the opportunity to explore vintage locomotives, passenger cars, cabooses, and more. Some of these trains are open for visitors to enter and explore.

Interactive Displays: Many exhibits are interactive, allowing visitors to engage with the history of railroads in a hands-on way. You can learn about the operation of steam engines, see how railway signals work, and gain insights into the life of railroad workers.

Historic Buildings: In addition to the roundhouse, the museum includes other historic buildings, such as a railway switch tower and a waiting room from a bygone era. These buildings provide a glimpse into the daily operations of the railway.

Special Events: The Minnesota Transportation Museum hosts special events and activities throughout the year. These events may include train rides, model railroad displays, educational programs, and seasonal celebrations.

Educational Programs: The museum offers educational programs for visitors of all ages. These programs may focus on the history of transportation, railroad safety, and the role of trains in shaping Minnesota's development.

Gift Shop: You can browse the museum's gift shop, which typically offers railroad-themed merchandise, books, and souvenirs.

Volunteer Opportunities: The museum often relies on volunteers to help with various aspects of its operations. If you have an interest in railroads and history, volunteering can be a rewarding way to get involved.

Membership: Consider becoming a member of the Minnesota Transportation Museum if you're a rail enthusiast or have a keen interest in transportation history. Membership often includes benefits such as free admission and special access to events.

Accessibility: The museum strives to be accessible to all visitors, and efforts are made to ensure that exhibits and facilities are wheelchair-friendly.

Plan Your Visit: Before visiting, check the museum's website for current hours of operation, admission fees, and any special exhibits or events. This will help you plan your visit accordingly.

A visit to the Minnesota Transportation Museum provides a captivating glimpse into the history of transportation in the state. Whether you have a passion for trains, a curiosity about history, or simply appreciate the significance of railways in shaping Minnesota's past, this museum offers an enriching and immersive experience.

107.Attend a live radio show taping at WCCO Radio.

Attending a live radio show taping at WCCO Radio in Minneapolis offers a unique behind-the-scenes experience of broadcast journalism and live radio production. Here's what you can expect when you participate in a live radio show taping:

Choosing a Show: WCCO Radio typically hosts a variety of radio shows covering news, talk, and other topics of interest. Check the station's schedule to choose a show that aligns with your interests.

Reservations: Some radio shows may require reservations or tickets for live audience participation. It's advisable to check the station's website or contact them in advance to inquire about reservations and availability.

Travel to Minneapolis Minnesota

Arrival: Arrive at the designated time and location for the live radio show taping. Be sure to arrive early to allow time for security checks and seating.

Audience Participation: Depending on the show, you may have the opportunity to be part of the live studio audience. In some cases, the show may involve interaction with the host or guests, such as asking questions or providing feedback.

Studio Tour: Before or after the taping, you may have the chance to take a tour of the radio station's studio facilities. This can provide valuable insights into the technical aspects of radio production.

Observation: As an audience member, you'll have the opportunity to observe the live broadcast process. You can see how radio hosts, producers, and technicians work together to create a radio show.

Broadcast Equipment: Radio studios are equipped with state-of-the-art technology, including microphones, soundboards, and editing software. Observing these tools in action can be fascinating.

Live Interviews: If the show features live interviews with guests, you can witness firsthand how hosts conduct interviews, ask questions, and engage with their subjects.

Broadcast Environment: Radio studios have a distinct atmosphere. You'll experience the energy, focus, and excitement that come with live broadcasting.

Recording: Keep in mind that radio shows are typically recorded for later broadcast, so there may be breaks, retakes, or edits during the taping.

Adherence to Rules: Be aware of any rules or guidelines provided by the radio station for audience members. This may include guidelines for appropriate behavior and audience participation.

Duration: The duration of the live radio show taping can vary depending on the show's format and content. Some shows may be relatively short, while others can last for several hours.

Appreciation for Broadcasting: Attending a live radio show taping offers a deeper appreciation for the world of broadcasting, journalism, and the work that goes into creating engaging and informative radio content.

Post-Show Interaction: After the taping, you may have the opportunity to interact with the hosts, guests, or station staff. It's a chance to ask questions, provide feedback, and connect with those involved in the production.

Attending a live radio show taping at WCCO Radio can be an enlightening and entertaining experience. Whether you're a radio enthusiast, a fan of the show, or simply curious about the inner workings of radio broadcasting, it's an opportunity to see the magic of live radio unfold in front of your eyes. Be sure to check the station's website or contact them for specific details, show schedules, and any audience participation guidelines.

108.Go on a brewery and distillery tour.

Embarking on a brewery and distillery tour in Minneapolis provides a delightful opportunity to explore the craft beverage scene and sample locally crafted beers and spirits. Here's what you can expect when you go on a brewery and distillery tour:

Tour Selection: Minneapolis boasts a diverse range of breweries and distilleries, each with its own unique offerings and ambiance. Research and choose a tour that aligns with your preferences, whether you're interested in craft beer, artisanal spirits, or both.

Reservations: Some brewery and distillery tours require advance reservations, especially if you plan to visit as part of a group or during peak hours. Check with the tour operator for availability and booking details.

Tour Guide: Upon arriving at the tour starting point, you'll likely be greeted by a knowledgeable tour guide or host who will lead you through the experience. They will provide insights into the history, production process, and the distinctive characteristics of the beverages.

Brewery Visit: If you're starting with a brewery tour, you'll get an insider's look at the brewing facilities. You'll learn about the brewing process, the ingredients used, and the equipment involved. Many tours include stops at various parts of the brewery, such as the brewhouse, fermentation tanks, and packaging areas.

Distillery Visit: For distillery tours, you'll have the opportunity to explore the distillation process, including the stills, barrels, and aging rooms. Guides will explain how different grains or ingredients are transformed into spirits like whiskey, vodka, or gin.

Tastings: The highlight of the tour is often the tastings. You'll sample a variety of beers or spirits produced by the brewery or distillery. This is a chance to savor the flavors, aromas, and nuances of the beverages. Some tours provide a guided tasting experience with a designated selection of drinks.

Souvenirs: Some tours include souvenirs like branded glassware, bottles, or merchandise. Check with the tour operator to see if any extras are included.

Pairing Experiences: Some tours offer food pairing experiences, where you can enjoy small bites or appetizers that complement the beverages. This can enhance the tasting experience.

Educational Insights: Throughout the tour, guides often share insights into the history, artistry, and science behind brewing and distilling. You'll gain a deeper appreciation for the craft.

Safety and Responsibility: Enjoy the tastings responsibly. If you're driving to the tour, designate a sober driver or use alternative transportation options to ensure everyone's safety.

Duration: The duration of brewery and distillery tours can vary, but they typically last around 1 to 2 hours. Longer tours or those involving multiple stops may take more time.

Age Restrictions: Be aware of age restrictions for tours and tastings. In the United States, you must be 21 or older to consume alcoholic beverages.

Tour Varieties: Minneapolis offers a variety of tour options, including walking tours, bus tours, and even brewery/distillery tours by bike or trolley. Choose the type of tour that suits your preferences.

Local Recommendations: Consider asking your tour guide for recommendations on other local breweries, distilleries, or dining options to explore after the tour.

A brewery and distillery tour in Minneapolis is not only an opportunity to sample fantastic craft beverages but also a chance to gain insights into the artistry and craftsmanship behind these products. Whether you're a beer aficionado, a spirits enthusiast, or simply looking for an enjoyable and educational experience, these tours offer a delightful way to savor the flavors of the city. Be sure to check with the specific tour operator for details, pricing, and reservations as you plan your brewery and distillery adventure.

109.Explore the Minnesota Landscape Arboretum in nearby Chanhassen.

Exploring the Minnesota Landscape Arboretum in nearby Chanhassen offers a serene and immersive experience in the natural world. Here's what you can expect when you visit this beautiful arboretum:

Location: The Minnesota Landscape Arboretum is located in Chanhassen, just a short drive from Minneapolis. It covers a vast area of natural beauty and meticulously curated gardens.

Landscape Diversity: The arboretum boasts a diverse array of landscapes, including lush gardens, woodlands, wetlands, prairies, and more. Each area is thoughtfully designed and maintained to showcase different ecosystems and plant species.

Gardens: The arboretum features numerous themed gardens, each with its own charm and character. Some notable gardens include the Rose Garden, Japanese Garden, Perennial Garden, and Butterfly Garden. Explore these spaces to appreciate the beauty of various flowers, trees, and shrubs.

Trails: There are miles of walking and hiking trails that wind through the arboretum's natural areas. These trails allow you to immerse yourself in the serene surroundings, observe wildlife, and enjoy the changing seasons.

Arboretum Collections: The arboretum is home to a diverse collection of plant species, including rare and endangered plants. You'll have the opportunity to discover and learn about a wide range of trees, shrubs, and flowers from around the world.

Education: The Minnesota Landscape Arboretum offers educational programs, workshops, and classes for visitors of all ages. These programs cover topics such as gardening, horticulture, and environmental conservation.

Events: Throughout the year, the arboretum hosts various events, seasonal celebrations, and art exhibitions. These events provide unique opportunities to engage with nature in creative and cultural ways.

Birdwatching: Bird enthusiasts will appreciate the abundant birdwatching opportunities at the arboretum. Bring your binoculars and look for native and migratory bird species that inhabit the area.

Photography: The beautiful and ever-changing landscapes make the arboretum a popular spot for photographers. Whether you're a professional or an amateur photographer, you'll find countless opportunities to capture stunning images.

Visitor Center: The visitor center provides information, maps, and resources to enhance your visit. It's a great starting point to plan your exploration of the arboretum.

Seasonal Beauty: The Minnesota Landscape Arboretum showcases different seasonal beauty throughout the year. Spring brings blooming flowers, while summer is a time of lush greenery. Fall foliage is stunning, and winter offers a peaceful, snow-covered landscape.

Accessibility: Efforts have been made to ensure that the arboretum is accessible to all visitors. Accessible paths and facilities are available for individuals with disabilities.

Picnicking: Many visitors choose to bring a picnic and enjoy a meal in the picturesque surroundings. Picnic areas are provided for your convenience.

Gift Shop: The arboretum often has a gift shop where you can purchase books, gardening tools, plants, and souvenirs related to horticulture and nature.

Membership: Consider becoming a member of the Minnesota Landscape Arboretum if you plan to visit frequently. Membership often includes benefits like free admission, discounts, and exclusive access to special events.

Plan Ahead: Before your visit, check the arboretum's website for current hours of operation, admission fees, and any special events or exhibitions that may be taking place.

Exploring the Minnesota Landscape Arboretum in Chanhassen offers a tranquil and educational experience in the heart of nature. Whether you're a nature enthusiast, a gardener, or simply seeking a peaceful escape from city life, this arboretum provides a breathtaking setting to connect with the natural world. Be sure to plan your visit according to your interests and the time of year to fully appreciate the beauty it offers.

110. Take a scenic river cruise on the Mississippi River.

Taking a scenic river cruise on the Mississippi River in Minneapolis is a relaxing and enjoyable way to appreciate the city's natural beauty and iconic landmarks. Here's what you can expect when you embark on a Mississippi River cruise:

Cruise Options: Several tour operators in Minneapolis offer Mississippi River cruises, each with its own unique features and offerings. You can choose from a variety of options, including narrated sightseeing tours, brunch or dinner cruises, and themed cruises.

Departure Locations: Most Mississippi River cruises depart from specific locations along the riverfront in downtown Minneapolis. Be sure to check the departure point of your chosen cruise when making reservations.

Sightseeing: The cruise provides a vantage point to admire Minneapolis from the water. You'll have stunning views of the city skyline, historic bridges, and riverside parks. The narrated tours often provide interesting facts and historical tidbits about the area.

Wildlife and Nature: While cruising, keep an eye out for wildlife such as bald eagles, waterfowl, and other creatures that call the river home. The Mississippi River is rich in natural beauty, and you may even spot some scenic bluffs along the shoreline.

Landmarks: Cruises typically pass by or near major Minneapolis landmarks, such as the Stone Arch Bridge, Guthrie Theater, Mill City Museum, and the historic district of St. Anthony Main. It's a great way to see these iconic sites from a different perspective.

Dining Options: Depending on the type of cruise, you may have dining options on board. Brunch and dinner cruises often include a meal, while sightseeing cruises may offer snacks and beverages for purchase.

Entertainment: Some cruises feature live entertainment, such as live music or storytelling, to enhance the experience and create a lively atmosphere.

Duration: The duration of a Mississippi River cruise can vary depending on the type of cruise you choose. Sightseeing cruises typically last around 90 minutes to 2 hours, while dining cruises may extend to 2-3 hours.

Seasonality: Be aware that cruise availability may vary by season. Cruises are more common in the warmer months, typically from spring to early fall. Check with the tour operator for their seasonal schedule.

Reservations: It's advisable to make reservations for your cruise, especially during peak times or for specialty cruises. Booking in advance ensures that you secure your spot.

Weather: Cruises are typically held rain or shine, but they may be affected by adverse weather conditions or high water levels. Check with the tour operator for their policy on weather-related cancellations.

Accessibility: Most cruise operators aim to provide accessible options for passengers with mobility needs. Be sure to inquire about accessibility when making reservations.

Photography: Don't forget your camera or smartphone to capture the scenic views and memorable moments during the cruise.

A scenic river cruise on the Mississippi River in Minneapolis offers a leisurely and picturesque way to explore the city's waterfront and enjoy its natural beauty. Whether you're a local resident or a visitor to Minneapolis, this experience allows you to relax, learn about the area, and appreciate the city's connection to the river. Be sure to check with the specific cruise operator for details, pricing, and reservations as you plan your river cruise adventure.

Conclusion

Minneapolis, Minnesota, is a rich and dynamic tapestry that has evolved from its indigenous roots to become a thriving and culturally diverse city. From its early days as a milling and lumber industry hub to its contemporary reputation as a vibrant metropolitan center, Minneapolis has experienced significant transformations and milestones that have shaped its identity.

The Dakota Sioux people were the original inhabitants of the area, and their presence is deeply ingrained in the city's history. The arrival of European settlers in the 19th century led to the establishment of milling operations along the Mississippi River, catapulting Minneapolis into a major milling and flour-producing center, earning it the moniker "Mill City."

The city's growth and prosperity were marked by innovations in industry and technology, exemplified by the creation of the iconic Stone Arch Bridge and the development of a bustling downtown area. However, this period of growth was also marked by social and labor challenges, including labor strikes and racial tensions, which left a lasting impact on the city's identity.

Minneapolis played a crucial role in the Civil Rights Movement, most notably as the birthplace of the American Indian Movement (AIM) and as the site of a pivotal desegregation lawsuit that paved the way for educational equality. In the late 20th century, Minneapolis emerged as a cultural and economic hub, known for its arts scene, thriving businesses, and a commitment to urban revitalization and sustainability.

Today, Minneapolis stands as a vibrant metropolis with a reputation for innovation, inclusivity, and natural beauty. Its modern identity is characterized by its commitment to social justice, environmental sustainability, and a diverse population. While the city has faced challenges, including issues related to racial equity and social disparities, it continues to work toward a more inclusive and equitable future.

In sum, the history of Minneapolis is a story of resilience, progress, and cultural diversity. From its early roots as a milling powerhouse to its present-day status as a city of arts, technology, and social progress, Minneapolis remains a place where history and innovation intersect, creating a dynamic and ever-evolving urban landscape.

Travel to Minneapolis Minnesota

If you enjoyed, please leave a 5-star Amazon Review

To get a free list of people who knows publishing top places to travel all around the world, click this link
https://bit.ly/peoplewhoknowtravel

References

Rcsprinter123, CC BY-SA 3.0 <https://creativecommons.org/licenses/by-sa/3.0>, via Wikimedia Commons
https://pixabay.com/photos/strawberry-dessert-strawberries-2191973/

Made in the USA
Middletown, DE
14 June 2024